HUMANIST VOICES IN UNITARIAN UNIVERSALISM

Kendyl L. R. Gibbons and William R. Murry, Editors

SKINNER HOUSE BOOKS

BOSTON

www.skinnerhouse.org

Printed in the United States
Cover and text design by Suzanne Morgan

print ISBN: 978-1-55896-783-0 / eBook ISBN: 978-1-55896-784-7
7 6 5 4 3 / 24 23 22 21 20

Library of Congress Cataloging-in-Publication Data

Names: Gibbons, Kendyl L. R., editor.
Title: Humanist voices in Unitarian Universalism / Kendyl L.R. Gibbons and
    William R. Murry, editors.
Description: Boston : Skinner House Books, 2016. | Includes bibliographical references.
Identifiers: LCCN 2016027001 (print) | LCCN 2016039272 (ebook) | ISBN
    9781558967830 (pbk. : alk. paper) | ISBN 9781558967847
Subjects: LCSH: Humanism. | Unitarian Universalist Association.
Classification: LCC BL2747.6 .H865 2016 (print) | LCC BL2747.6 (ebook) | DDC
    289.1/32—dc23
LC record available at https://lccn.loc.gov/2016027001

"Black Humanism's Response to Suffering" by Colin Bossen was first published in *UU World*, Summer 2010, reprinted with permission; "Love Your Neighbor First, Not Second" by Doug Muder was first published in UUWorld.org on May 23, 2016, reprinted with permission; The excerpt from the poem "Loving Humans" by Alice Walker is from the book *Hard Times Require Furious Dancing*, copyright © 2010 by Alice Walker, reprinted with permission of New World Library, Novato CA, www.newworldlibrary.com.

CONTENTS

HUMANISM AND RELIGIOUS EDUCATION

THE IMPORTANCE OF COMMUNITY

INTRODUCTION

Humanists agree on many things, but Humanism includes a variety of aspects, and it means different things to different people, depending on which aspect a particular Humanist chooses to emphasize. Amid this diversity, the contributors to this book agree that Humanism is not primarily about denying the existence of the supernatural but about affirming positive values, especially the worth and dignity of every human being, the centrality of social justice, and the importance of community. They also agree that Humanism leads to a way of living that is morally responsible, meaningful, and joyful and that seeks to make the world a better place. The authors totally reject the erroneous idea that Humanists are immoral and irresponsible.

In a sermon, Nancy McDonald Ladd, minister at the River Road Unitarian Universalist Congregation in Bethesda, Maryland, offered a valuable distinction between the theistic and Humanist perspectives. She noted that the

Unitarian Universalist Christian minister Carl Scovel wrote that "the Great Surmise was simply this: 'that at the heart of all creation lies a good intent, a purposeful goodness, from which we come, by which we live our fullest, to which we shall at last return. And that this—this deep well of purposeful goodness—is the supreme reality of our lives.'"

Scovel's words represent a beautiful and accurate statement of the central meaning of the Christian faith. Ladd, however, offered her own view, and although she does not use the word *Humanism*, her ideas are a superb statement of a Humanist perspective:

> Lately I have pondered a different surmise. Not to live as if we are loved beyond measure. But to live as if we ourselves are capable of loving beyond measure, no matter what. Can I prove this is true? . . . No. Most of the evidence probably points to the contrary, in fact.
>
> I cannot prove that we are capable of loving beyond measure even in the direst of circumstances, . . . but I choose to live as if it is possible.

The Humanist does not find evidence of a goodness at the heart of creation. We Humanists believe the universe is indifferent to human life, and we have no experience of being loved beyond measure by a goodness at the heart of things. But we do believe that human beings are of great worth and dignity and that we are capable of loving and doing good and that we can make our lives meaningful and the world a better place.

This book is about religious Humanism, but there is also secular Humanism, and people often ask about the difference between them. The two philosophies share the same basic convictions, but religious Humanists emphasize the importance of coming together as a community of people with similar beliefs and values, whereas secular Humanists generally do not. For this reason, some refer to religious Humanism as congregational Humanism because of their concern that the word *religious* connotes belief in the supernatural. Religious Humanists also value sharing feelings and emotions more than secular Humanists do. As the percentage of the population that claims no religious identity increases, the enduring message of Humanism prepares to speak to a new generation, offering a community of intellectual integrity, evolving conscience, creative endeavor, and the celebration of human life and human connection.

Both editors of this collection identify as religious Humanists, and both of us are Unitarian Universalist ministers.

In assembling this volume, we identified seven themes among the contributions, and the text is divided accordingly. There is some overlap, since each essay addresses more than one aspect of Humanism. All the essays reflect a nontheistic, naturalistic perspective and explore the role of this viewpoint within Unitarian Universalism.

The first section, "History and Core Beliefs," consists of introductory thoughts by the editors: One essay looks at the history of religious Humanism, and the other examines its core convictions. For many Humanists, the meaning of

Humanism centers on certain beliefs about life and the world; the essays with this emphasis are grouped together in the second section, "What Humanists Stand For." The third section, "Humanism Is About How We Live," discusses Humanism as a way of approaching life and living well, rather than as a set of beliefs. In the fourth section, "Humanism and Unitarian Universalist Diversity," the writers grapple with diversity within Humanism and express both their concerns and their hopes for the future of Humanism within the diversity of the Unitarian Universalist Association. Several contributors understand Humanism primarily as emphasizing social justice and the effort to make a difference in the world; their essays appear in the next section, "Humanism and Social Action." The sixth section deals with Humanism and religious education. And the last section, "The Importance of Community," emphasizes the ways in which a strong sense of community distinguishes religious Humanism from secular Humanism.

We capitalize the terms Humanism and Humanists because, in our view, Humanism is a bona fide spiritual path in the same way as are the other "isms" in this Voices series—Judaism, Christianity, and Buddhism. Although Humanism is not yet recognized as a world religion, it has millions of adherents and has been a major part of Unitarian Universalism for a hundred years.

As editors, we are very grateful to each author for their thoughtful essay; every essay is an important contribution to the diversity of this joyous and responsible way of living and believing that we call religious Humanism.

HISTORY AND CORE BELIEFS

ONE HUNDRED YEARS OF
UNITARIAN UNIVERSALIST HUMANISM

WILLIAM R. MURRY

Humanism in various forms has a long history dating back to ancient India and China and, in the West, to ancient Greece especially. It can be seen as having three interwoven strands: a scientific curiosity about the origins of the universe; a commitment to human happiness and the common good; and a sense of skepticism, or a denial of claims, about the supernatural. Several pre-Socratic philosophers, Thales, Anaximander, Xenophanes, and Heraclitus, were philosophical materialists who questioned the existence of the gods. Xenophanes, like Ludwig Feuerbach in the nineteenth century, believed that the gods were a human creation. He suggested that if horses could draw their gods, they would look like horses. Materialists Democritus and, later, Epicurus developed the theory that everything is composed of atoms, and Protagoras famously asserted that "man is the measure of all things." The foundations of Western Humanism, like so many other religious and philosophic ideas, were laid in pre-Christian Greece.

But with its emphasis on applying reason and critical thinking to all areas of life, the eighteenth-century European Enlightenment provided the philosophical basis for modern Humanism. The French philosophers like Voltaire and Diderot used reason to attack superstition, bigotry, intolerance, and religious fanaticism, all of which they considered the chief obstacles to free thought and social reform. They and other Enlightenment thinkers such as the English philosophers David Hume and Adam Smith believed that the application of reason and scientific thinking to human concerns and problems would improve human life much more than religion could. Because Enlightenment figures did not spare religious doctrines from reason and critical thinking, there was a good deal of skepticism about such Christian notions as the divinity of Jesus, the trinity, the resurrection of Jesus, and even the idea of a supernatural God. Many of America's founders were deeply influenced by this kind of thinking, which led many of them to embrace a Deistic idea of God rather than the traditional Christian understanding of a personal deity who answers prayers and acts in history.

In early nineteenth-century America, skepticism about Christian doctrines produced such freethinkers as Frances (Fanny) Wright, Elizabeth Cady Stanton, the openly atheistic Ernestine L. Rose, and Robert G. Ingersoll, known as "the Great Agnostic." Ingersoll lectured tirelessly around the country, rejecting supernatural religion but arguing for a "religion of humanity," which we today call Humanism. Stanton thought Christianity was responsible for the subjugation of women, and she embraced the idea of a religion of humanity. Especially interesting is the Polish-born Rose, who concluded her eloquent 1861 lecture, "A Defense of Atheism," with these words:

> Though I cannot believe in your God whom you have failed to demonstrate, I believe in man; if I have no faith in your religion, I have faith—unbounded, unshaken faith—in the principles of right, of justice, and humanity. Whatever good you are willing to do for the sake of your god, I am full as willing to do for the sake of man. . . . Whatever good you would do out of fear of punishment, or hope of reward hereafter, the Atheist would do simply because it is good; and being so he would receive the far surer and more certain reward, springing from well-doing, which would constitute his pleasure, and promote his happiness.

Meanwhile, literary and archeological biblical scholarship began to cast doubt on the historical authenticity of much of Western Scripture. All of this laid a firm foundation for the emergence of religious Humanism in the early twentieth century.

Explicit Unitarian Universalist Humanism began during World War I, when two Unitarian ministers, John Dietrich and Curtis Reese, began to preach and teach a religion without God. Reese called it a religion of democracy, and Dietrich called it Humanism. They advocated social change as well as freedom of belief. Conservatives in the Unitarian movement fought their views, and in the 1920s, a serious controversy took place between the Humanists and the theists, both at the General Assembly (then called the May Meetings) and in Unitarian publications. However, since Unitarianism had no creed, Dietrich and Reese prevailed, and religious Humanism became a significant part of the Unitarian movement. Also in the 1920s, a number of ministerial students at the University of Chicago and its Unitarian affiliate, Meadville Theological School, embraced the new ideas of religious Humanism. They were no doubt influenced by a very liberal faculty at the divinity school of the University of Chicago, especially by A. Eustace Haydon, professor of comparative religion there and a leading Humanist. In 1933, the students organized the new Humanist Fellowship and decided there ought to be a statement summarizing the beliefs of religious . Humanism. They asked University of Michigan philosopher and Unitarian layman Roy Wood Sellars to draft such a statement, which was published in 1933 as "The Humanist Manifesto." It was signed by thirty-four of the day's leading philosophers and Unitarian ministers, including John Dewey, as well as Dietrich and Reese.

The manifesto proclaimed Humanism as a vital new religious alternative for the twentieth century and began with the following declaration:

The time has come for widespread recognition of the radical changes in religious beliefs throughout the modern world. The time is past for mere revision of traditional attitudes. Science and economic change have disrupted the old beliefs. Religions the world over are under the necessity of coming to terms with new conditions created by a vastly increased knowledge and experience. In every field of human activity the vital movement is now in the direction of a candid and explicit humanism.

The manifesto went on to set forth the basic Humanist beliefs: The natural universe is all there is; there is no supernatural realm; the universe is "self-existing and not created"; human beings evolved as part of nature (an affirmation of biological evolution); and religion and human culture are the creations of humankind, not a result of divine revelation. It maintained that ethics and values spring from human experience and reflection, and emphasized "the complete realization of human personality" as the highest goal to be sought in the one life we have. It argued for the enhancement of human life through democracy and a more equitable distribution of wealth and expressed a preference for a "socialized and cooperative" economy to accomplish that. It concluded with these words:

Though we consider the religious forms and ideas of our fathers no longer adequate, the quest for the good life is still the central task for mankind. Man is at last becoming aware that he alone is responsible for the realization of the world of his dreams, that he has within himself the power for its achievement. He must set intelligence and will to the task.

Religious Humanism has changed in several of its details since 1933, but not in its basic ideas. Today it can speak of a naturalistic spirituality; it addresses environmental pollution and the danger of climate change, issues not on the minds of people at earlier times. And it has embraced feminist issues such as reproductive rights and women's equality, as well as gender-neutral language, and rights—including marriage—for lesbian, gay, bisexual, and transgender people.

Unitarian Humanists founded the American Humanist Association in 1941. Today it provides a home mainly for secular Humanists, whereas the Unitarian Universalist Association continues to include both religious and secular Humanists. In 1973, the American Humanist Association published a second Humanist Manifesto and thirty years later issued the statement "Humanism and Its Aspirations: Humanist Manifesto III"—which was signed by eleven Unitarian Universalist ministers, including the co-editors of this book.

Each manifesto uses language and ideas that reflect its own time and incorporate contemporary social concerns. The 2003 document includes these words that epitomize both religious and secular Humanism: "The lifestance of

Humanism—guided by reason, inspired by compassion, and informed by experience—encourages us to live life well and fully." The Unitarian Universalist Humanist Association, a group of several hundred UU volunteers, identifies reason, compassion, and community as the essence of religious Humanism.

Both manifestos articulate the essential core of Humanism: a religious perspective that is grounded in the natural, not the supernatural; that emphasizes the worth and dignity of human beings rather than the glory of God; and that considers social justice and social responsibility to be far more important than personal piety.

—◦—

WILLIAM R. (BILL) MURRY *is minister emeritus of the River Road Unitarian Universalist Congregation of Bethesda, Maryland, past president of Meadville Lombard Theological School, and the author of three books and several articles on religious Humanism. He is also a former college professor and college chaplain.*

ESSENTIALS OF HUMANISM

KENDYL L. R. GIBBONS

Let's begin with a clarification and what is perhaps a controversial claim. While the terms *atheist* and *Humanist* are often used interchangeably, they are not, in fact, synonymous. A person can certainly be an atheist without embracing any of the commitments of Humanism, and a person could also maintain a position of indifference about the possible existence of supernatural beings and still live with integrity as a Humanist. As a religious position and a spiritual path, Humanism looks beyond the idea that a self-conscious, personal god doesn't exist. Rather, Humanism is founded on the much more radical claim that the existence or nonexistence of such a god, or goddess, or gods, does not matter much. As its name implies, Humanism is concerned with the world of human existence as it is known through human experience.

The question of god, while potentially interesting in some ways, is secondary, and many practicing Humanists have differed, and do differ, concerning it. On what seems like good evidence to them, some Humanists are persuaded that the existence of a self-conscious, personal deity is clearly impossible. Others take a position of intellectual modesty, which holds that there is insufficient evidence for us as human beings to know whether gods exist. Others, good Humanists still, have had experiences that would make them think that perhaps there is some kind of larger being at the heart of the universe. Several versions of the-istic Humanism regard a supernatural being as concerned with the quality of human life, and they demand that god's would-be followers must work for human betterment. Yet, in the end, what all of these types of Humanists have in common is far more significant than their diversity on this question.

In any form, Humanism clearly denies any authority in direct divine revelation. This stance distinguishes it from other religious positions. Whether or not the gods exist isn't all that important, because we as Humanists would not take these spiritual entities' word for anything. What we are willing to say about the universe and our lives is based exclusively on our own shared experience and reason. "Because the Bible tells me so"—or the Quran, or Jesus, or Jehovah, or the Buddha, or any other religious authority—carries no weight with a Humanist.

We trust that which can be proven, either by evidence, science, and careful study or by the cumulative moral insight and experience of the human race. The attempt to make any collection of ideas—ideas that necessarily have their origins in some human mind—into sacred scripture supposedly revealed by the gods and thus above all criticism is what Humanists consistently reject. Thus the gods' existence or nonexistence is of minor importance, for they are of no help to us in any case.

Humanism begins with the premise that our human bodies and minds are the tools with which we must engage this world and our existence. As the late Unitarian Universalist minister Forrest Church observed, we must come to terms with the twin realities of being alive and having to die. The Humanist philosopher and hymnist Ken Patton puts it more poetically: "Without any say in the matter, we are born, and without vote or rebuttal, we die." These two facts are the givens of human experience, and the question is, then, how will we respond to this situation?

On the one hand, we could spend whatever time of awareness that we may have on this planet sulking because the conditions of life are not more to our liking. We can search, futilely, as far as anyone has ever been able to determine, for the antidote to death, refusing to acknowledge the necessity of our mortality. Or perhaps we could drown that awareness in the chemistry of our brains with alcohol or drugs or other perception-altering practices. We can, in essence, reject the life that we are given and die in bitterness if we choose.

On the other hand, we can take the knowledge of our impending death as a motive to run around frantically, grasping and seizing whatever immediate gratifications come our way as if every instant excitement or pleasure might be our last. We can try to experience the least possible pain and the greatest possible entertainment, using blind impulse, and live a life of selfish and superficial enjoyment. We can try such a life, even though many generations of experimentation have shown that such pleasures usually burn themselves out quickly, leaving jaded disillusionment in their wake.

Standing in opposition to these two fundamentally immature reactions, the faith of Humanism, as an authentic spiritual path, invites us to grow up. We can consider thoughtfully what might constitute a good life, a life worth living even in the face of certain death, and then try such an approach, always leaving room for the fruits of both reason and experience to correct our course. As Patton concludes, "Our only wisdom is to bestow ourselves on the universe which upholds us, and to accept the necessity of its ways." All religious experience, traditions, and institutions are necessarily human experience, traditions, and institutions. From this perspective, all religions have their origins in the question of what it means to live well, to live a good life.

Some religions answer that question by supposing that our current lives in this world are simply preparation for other, future states of existence, so that what constitutes living well now is whatever will pay off in the greatest happiness and pleasure in the hereafter. Again, Humanism is concerned not so much with whether there is another world, but with how much time and energy we invest in preparing for it. Many of us suppose that our state of consciousness after the body's death will be just what it was before the body's conception: nonexistent. Others suppose that we cannot know the answer to this mystery, since no evidence seems sufficient either way. A few of us have had uncanny personal experiences that incline us to think there may be something more beyond this life. But if we primarily focus on what makes a good life here and now, we are called on to do our best to do what is right in this world. If some future state were to exist, its moral laws might be the same as those that pertain to this one, and we would be inclined to do what we are doing, anyway.

Alternatively, some separate moral system would invite us to do what is wrong as we understand it now, to build up points for the future. It is this possibility that Humanism vigorously rejects. We are asked to do what is right and to accept the consequences of our actions in the world in which we are now living. We are not to be bribed with promises of rewards, or intimidated with threats, into doing what we know here and now to be wrong. If it turns out that I have been mistaken in my guess, and in fact there is some judgment that follows my death, I choose to deal with it when it comes, in the confidence of having done the best I could with this life as I understood it. As Henry David Thoreau is said to have responded on his death bed, "One world at a time, my friend; one world at a time."

Humanism rejects suppositions about a possible life to come as a source of knowledge about what makes our present choices good, but it very intentionally accepts the reality of death as part of what makes the task of learning to be human urgent and compelling. Knowing that we are mortal and that our time is limited suggests that, to figure out how to live well, we must start now; there is no time to waste feeling sorry for ourselves or playing around with trifles. In this respect, Humanism is a demanding spiritual path. It teaches that we are accountable, individually and collectively, for what we make of ourselves and our world. No tolerant parent is going to appear in the last act to straighten out the messes we have made, either in our relationships or on the globe. No divine puppeteer is pulling the strings that cause us to dance; we are free to choose among all the options we can discover or invent, and then we and everyone else must live with the results of our choices. And thus by their consequences, for ourselves and others, must our choices be evaluated.

The sternness of Humanism lies in its teaching that we must not wait to be rescued or excused. The operation of cause and effect is never suspended in this world by special pleading, no matter how earnest. We are called to spiritual maturity, which means to submit as gracefully as we can to reality, to both the logic and the arbitrariness of the universe as it happens to exist. We may, of course, strive to change those realities through the application of intelligence, effort, and the principles by which the universe itself operates.

Much of human progress has occurred from the determination of our ancestors to understand why the world is the way it is and, after learning how it might be changed, changing it. There is nothing to stop us from eradicating diseases if we can find effective vaccinations. We are free to cross the oceans if we can discover the principles of navigation. Presumably, we might lift the ancient curses of hunger or warfare from the human race if we had the knowledge and the will.

The good news of Humanism is that the well-being of this planet, and of our community most widely conceived, is the good we are driven to seek. We are not fundamentally deceived; there is no arbitrary obedience required of us against our own common sense. We have, of course, made both individual and collective mistakes from time to time. As we learn to understand ourselves and our world better, the knowledge that we could make yet more mistakes should help us cultivate a certain humility in our assertions about what we know. Nevertheless, our deepest joy is trustworthy, and what sustains us in shared happiness and comfort is a fair guide to what it ultimately means to live well.

Humanism as a spiritual path invites us to aspire to pleasures that are deeper and more lasting than those of a juvenile hedonism. It begins with the understanding that no human being can be fully happy at the expense of another, or even in the knowledge of another's misery. Until all people have the opportunity to participate in creating for themselves good lives, as they would define them, none of us is as happy as we might be. The suffering of others always diminishes our own pleasures, for we are social creatures, designed by evolution to reflect one another's experiences in our own perceptions. A thoughtless grasping for selfish indulgences cannot make a satisfying life in the long run.

Another principle that Humanism invites us to grasp is the recognition that the deepest and most enduring pleasures require cultivation. By investing patience, practice, and self-discipline, we can learn skills that make life more rewarding, whether we become better hockey players, more expressive water colorists, better parents, more appreciative readers, better cooks, more precise scientists . . . the list is endless. The point is that we may choose to sacrifice immediate gratification in the service of a greater fulfillment later on, and the good life is one in which immediate pleasures are thoughtfully balanced with the cultivation of lasting happiness. The more you take time to know and understand human nature and the nature of the world, the more likely you are to be effective in making your life what you most truly want it to be. And of course, the good life is also one in which our vision of what constitutes the good life itself matures and expands and grows deeper over time. To engage in the kind of self-examination and reflection that is required for such intellectual, emotional, and moral development is part of what it means to practice Humanism.

Humanism also affirms that this world is the kind of place in which the resources that we need for understanding and creating good lives are indeed available to us. We can live well, if we will go about it with persistence, humility, reason, and integrity. This belief is, incidentally, quite the opposite of a religion or philosophy that teaches, as some would say, that we can believe anything we want. In fact, as the third Manifesto asserts, Humanism encourages us to "distinguish things as they are from things as we might wish or imagine them to be." Or, as Patton says, "Our brains are unhitched from our longings. . . . Our eyes will not lie to us on demand."

There are many things that I would like to believe. Some of them are very delightful ideas. Unhappily, evidence indicates that many of these things are not true. Therefore, as a Humanist, I am called on to regard them as lovely images, not as truth, no matter how much I want to believe them. This commitment to reality and the authority of evidence is one of the most central disciplines of Humanism.

But for all its celebration of our intellectual capacity to understand the world and ourselves, Humanism is not just a function of the mind. The life well lived has emotional, aesthetic, and moral fulfillment as well as mental and physical satisfaction, and these we ignore at our peril. Love for those closest to us and compassion for all creatures, the capacity to be touched by beauty and repulsed by ugliness, and the longing for justice in the world and honor in oneself are as essential to spiritual maturity and lasting happiness as is intellectual reason or physical health. Each of these dimensions has its own perspective on truth and is not subsumed by the others. Reasoning will not make right what is wrong, nor make what is hideous lovely. Nor will it make us love the person our heart shrinks from. We can certainly learn to see more clearly the moral subtleties of a situation, to appreciate harmonies of color and form in unlikely places, and to hold in esteem people we weren't initially attracted to, just as we can also condition our bodies and educate our minds. But this is a process of cultivation, not contradiction. Humanism asks us to attend to all of our faculties and to recognize that a life can only be truly well lived when it has developed satisfaction in all of these aspects.

In the end, Humanism is not a faith for the mindless, the heartless, those without integrity, or those who are merely cynical in their skepticism. It is not a feather bed for the spiritually lazy who want to believe and do as little as possible with their all-too-brief, mortal lives. Humanism encourages those of us who embrace it to live as fully as we can, in all the authentic wonder and curiosity that the human spirit can generate. It summons us to a persistent obedience to evidence and reason, to recognize in our deepest and most beautiful longings not the world that is, but the world that might be, if we, by our courage, intelligence, and dedication, will make it so.

Humanism invites us into compassionate connection with others, so that we may build the common good and, in that enterprise, make our own days glad. It offers us no assurances of divine love or a life to come, but rather the assurance that this life matters, that we create our meaning here and now, in this very world. It teaches us to find our satisfactions in work and service, rest and love, and to accept our fears and failures for what we may learn from them.

And, by no means least of all, Humanism summons us to gratitude, not because some judging deity needs its ego stroked, but because that is how we become most fully human. To live well is to live with intelligence and integrity, with justice and compassion, with wholeness and beauty, and, finally, inevitably, with thanks and praise, for all that is our fragile, tragic, precious life.

—◦—

KENDYL L. R. GIBBONS *is minister of All Souls Unitarian Church, Kansas City, Missouri. She is a past president of the Unitarian Universalist Ministers Association, a former co-dean of the Humanist Institute, and has also served as minister of the First Unitarian Society of Minneapolis and the DuPage Unitarian Universalist Church of Naperville, Illinois. She has also taught courses on worship and preaching at Meadville Lombard Theological School.*

WHAT HUMANISTS STAND FOR

WHOLE-PERSON HUMANISM

JOHN B. HOOPER

When I was five years old, my mother always told me that happiness was the key to life. When I went to school, they asked me what I wanted to be when I grew up. I wrote down "happy." They told me I didn't understand the assignment, and I told them they didn't understand life.

—Anonymous

Humanists have long recognized that the pursuit of happiness is inextricably connected to the pursuit of truth, peace, and justice.

We humans are deeply imbedded in our world. Even the use of the word environment implies too great a separation between ourselves and the rest of existence. We relate to the world around us in three interconnected ways. We directly experience (feel) it with our senses—the so-called first-person mode. We also interact with others both verbally and nonverbally—the second person. Finally, we observe the world around us, gaining an understanding of the universe and our place in it—the third person. Science, of course, functions with a third-person perspective. But we need to remember that scientific explanation is the map, not the territory. As each of us experiences life, all three existential modes of relating to the world happen simultaneously, continuously generating the thoughts and feelings that define our inner life.

Over the past several decades, there have been enormous advances in what may be called the sciences of experience. We now know that we are essentially hardwired for empathy and compassion. Our brains did not evolve to enable us to think, but rather to help us live our lives. Cognitive scientists have shown that emotions and feelings are not derived from thought. In *The Feeling of What Happens*, Antonio Damasio says our feelings are an important component in how we "make our way in the world." To realize the full potential of our humanity as individuals and as communities, we must pay close attention to all three of the relational mechanisms that define our lives. And we must work to strike the appropriate balance among them. This is what I call becoming a whole-person Humanist.

Problems arise when one mode of relating is given undue preference over the others. We can see this clearly when we look at religion. Religious fundamentalists of all types focus on first-person beliefs and feelings and divide the world into believers and nonbelievers. They have little or no tolerance for third-person analysis of their beliefs. However, at the other end of the religious spectrum—or should I say the nonreligious end of the social spectrum—there are the secularists who are skeptical of feelings and beliefs and who promote science and critical thinking as the most appropriate ways to appreciate existence. At the extreme end of the secularists are the rigid atheists who strive for the elimination of religion in all its forms. They tend to divide humanity into the rational and the irrational. The anti-religionists overemphasize the third-person analytical perspective, and the fundamentalists overemphasize the first-person experiential perspective.

This leaves a lot of room for all those, including Unitarian Universalists, who are situated somewhere between the religious fundamentalists and the rigid atheists on the ideological spectrum. Humanists who are mainly secular, such as the members of the American Humanist Association, and Humanists who are Unitarian Universalists, operate under the principles of whole-person Humanism.

Last year, I attended a lecture by the famous primatologist Frans de Waal and author of *The Bonobo and the Atheist*. When de Waal was asked about his own life stance, he said he considered himself an "apatheist." God or no God, it just doesn't matter. The primatologist's position makes some sort of sense. Why waste time arguing about the existence of God? Let's just live our lives as if we—individually and collectively—are responsible for what we make of them, because there is absolutely no reason to believe otherwise.

Most Unitarian Universalists are theological apatheists most of the time. Indeed, a 2005 Unitarian Universalist Association Commission on Appraisal report said the results of several surveys suggest that 65 to 84 percent of Unitarian Universalists do not make the "transcendental dimension assumption" whether or not they call it "God." Being theological apatheists does not mean we UUs are apathetic about anything else. The UU seven Principles call us to a life of action infused with love and reason—a whole-person life. The same goes for the secular Humanists. Bette Chambers, former president of the American Humanist Association, makes the case for Humanism this way:

> Humanism is the light of my life and the fire in my soul. It is the deep-felt conviction, in every fiber of my being, that human love is a power far transcending the relentless, onward rush of our largely deterministic cosmos. All human life must seek a reason for existence within the bounds of an uncaring physical world, and it is love coupled with empathy, democracy, and a commitment to selfless service which undergirds the faith of a Humanist.

These are exciting times for Unitarian Universalists and for Humanists. While many of our fellow Americans are clinging to the literalist beliefs of the past and others are attempting to construct a life according to the rejection of those beliefs, a growing number of us are looking for a way that works better for us. Before I go into this third way, let me tell you briefly about my own background and how I came to be a Humanist Unitarian Universalist.

Raised Episcopalian, I was especially drawn to the resonance of the Anglican music and to the community experience of liturgical ritual. I sang in the choir and then became an acolyte (or "altar boy"), rising to become head acolyte in my late teens. I had made up my mind to become an Episcopal priest until something abruptly changed the course of my life.

One Sunday, after doing my head-acolyte thing of carrying the cross at the front of the procession up to the chancel, I settled in for yet another worship service. While I was watching the faithful filing up to the altar rail to receive communion, it struck me: This doesn't make sense to me anymore. I didn't believe any of it, and if I were to be honest with myself, I probably hadn't for some time. Not only did I know it in my mind, but I also felt it in the core of my being. I felt a rush of realization. There is no God watching out for or watching over me. I felt a sudden exhilarating and frightening sense of freedom. My life is my own to do with what I will. It was like being born again in a weird sort of way.

I loved the freedom that casting off all supernatural crutches gave me. I began carrying pocket editions of the writings of Bertrand Russell and Friedrich Nietzsche around with me and quoting from them to any unsuspecting victim who would listen. I had the same level of enthusiasm for my newfound atheism that is exhibited by today's young freethinkers, who relish the writings of the "new atheists." I was a committed atheist/agnostic and existentialist long before I became a Unitarian Universalist.

Of course, this change significantly dampened my priestly ambitions. Since math and science came naturally to me, I studied chemistry in college and graduate school and became a scientist—almost by default. I had left organized religion and become a none—the term that is now used to refer to that ever-growing class of people who say they have no religious affiliation.

The nones have received much attention recently. "America's Changing Religious Landscape," a 2015 report on surveys on the religious affiliations of Americans by the Pew Forum on Religion and Public Life, reveals a potential challenge and opportunity for Humanism and for Unitarian Universalism:

> Around 22 percent of the U.S. public are religiously unaffiliated today. The growth in the number of religiously unaffiliated Americans—sometimes called the rise of the "nones"—is largely driven by generational replacement, the gradual supplanting of older generations by newer ones. A third of adults under 30 have no religious affiliation, compared with just one in ten who are 65 and older.

The ranks of the mainline denominations become more depleted every year. The challenge for Unitarian Universalism is to be perceived as not just another organized religion. If Unitarian Universalism is framed that way, our numbers may not stay level, but will probably drop precipitously. Younger people in particular are looking for new ways to come together in community outside of the traditional religious model. And this is where the opportunity lies. We can offer them opportunities for deep interpersonal interactions. Moreover, we have not been, and are not now, a traditional religion.

Like many others, when I finally found Unitarian Universalism after wandering around in Noneville for twenty-five years, it felt like coming home. Several aspects of Unitarian Universalism in particular drew me to this way of life. It is a religion of freedom and responsibility, not creeds—one could be an atheist or an agnostic and, as a UU, still be religious! Moreover, Unitarian Universalism is concerned with life before death, not with any postulated hereafter—the seven Principles are about action, not belief. Finally, Unitarian Universalism provides a beloved community that encourages its members to exercise compassion driven by rational analysis.

In short, I was drawn by what I now know is the Humanistic core of Unitarian Universalism. And this brings me to that third way, which transcends the true-believer-versus-atheist dichotomy that I mentioned earlier. If whole-person UU Humanism is presented in the right form—outside of the traditional congregational assembly—it will appeal to a large fraction of today's young nones.

Many Humanists are concerned that the increasing use of God language in some Unitarian Universalist worship services undermines our message and may actually turn off many nonaffiliated visitors, who otherwise might be attracted to Unitarian Universalism. UU congregations need to address this concern because these newcomers probably won't stick around long enough to adopt a more metaphorical interpretation of the language of reverence. Of course, there may also be other newcomers who feel there is not enough of such language. However, UU congregations and communities are still the best game in town for people who are looking for authenticity, acceptance, and love in a dogma-free community.

Today's nones are not monolithic, but many of them are very uncomfortable with traditional religious language and practices. They tend to avoid the major organized religions—indeed some of them would say that they are "recovering" from one of these religions. At the same time, many nones affirm belief in God, and some of these would probably fit in a theistic or pluralist Unitarian Universalist congregation, while others might find a positive Humanism to be compatible with their views if they really understood it. The popular writings of the "new atheists" have equated the word religion with belief in God, and yet as André Comte-Sponville says in his *Little Book of Atheist Spirituality*, "all theisms are religious, but not all religions are theistic." It is possible that, like Frans de Waal, many of both secular Humanists and Unitarian Universalists are simply indifferent to most popular concepts of God.

In *The Daemon Knows: Literary Greatness and the American Sublime*, literary critic and scholar Harold Bloom concludes from his exhaustive study of "the American Religion" that religion is the poetry of the people, as opposed to the opiate of the people, as Karl Marx called it. We congregational Humanists need to express an affective poetry of reality if we really want to capture the hearts and minds of today's nontheistic spiritual seekers. We may be able to reach the mind with scientific arguments, but we need poetry to reach the heart.

One of the most exciting recent developments in American secularism is that atheists and secular Humanists are realizing the importance of second-person Humanism—the need for human interaction and for building networks of connection and support. As a result, they are forming congregations or communities themselves. Greg Epstein, the Humanist chaplain at Harvard University, puts it this way in his recent book *Good Without God*:

> The single biggest weakness of modern, organized atheism and Humanism . . . has been the movement's own tendency to focus on religious beliefs, when the key to understanding religion lies not in belief at all but in practice—in what people do, not just what they think. . . . [N]ow we need to sing and to build. We need to acknowledge that as nonreligious people, we may not need God or miracles, but we are human, and we do need the experiential things—the

heart—that religion provides: some form of ritual, culture, and community.

Unfortunately, however, in this age of instant communication and 24-7 news cycles, the people at the extremes seem to get most of the attention. The doctrinaire atheists and the religious fundamentalists each paint a picture that doesn't include most Humanists, and certainly not most Unitarian Universalists. Secular and religious Humanists need to work together to provide places for the nones to feel at home. The Unitarian Universalist Humanist Association has set its main mission as building bridges between the secular community, especially the nones, and Unitarian Universalism.

Why should people who have come to distrust organized religion be attracted to Unitarian Universalism? One is tempted to reply, "Well, we UUs have never been accused of being organized!" But the real attraction that religiously nonaffiliated seekers could feel for Unitarian Universalism is that they could be embraced by a community of open-minded, warm-hearted people more like them than they could have possibly believed.

A personal experience showed me how important it is to be part of a supportive, loving community. On September 13, 2001, I attended the weekly choir rehearsal at the Unitarian Church in Westport, Connecticut. We had learned that two sons of one of our choir members had been at work at Cantor Fitzgerald, located in the World

Trade Center, when the twin towers fell two days before, and were among the missing. We stood in silence, embracing one another with tears in our eyes not knowing what to say, when one of the sopranos began singing with a broken, almost imperceptible voice. One by one we each joined in until the room was filled with the sounds of the hymn: "We are a gentle, angry people and we are singing, singing for our lives." In that moment, I felt that there was no other place where I would rather have been and no other people with whom I would rather be than my own beloved Unitarian Universalist community.

Unitarian Universalists have a special role to play in the emerging post-denominational age. The American form of Humanism began a century ago within our Unitarian tradition. Half the signers of the 1933 Humanist Manifesto were Unitarian scholars or ministers or both, and the manifesto captured the imagination of freethinking students. I believe that, like our forebears, we Unitarian Universalists have a special obligation to the freethinking young people of today. We must accept them where they are in their life journeys. Our congregations need to be as openly welcoming to atheists and agnostics as they are to other socially marginalized people. Young nonbelievers of today shouldn't have to wait twenty-five years to come home to Unitarian Universalism as I did—or perhaps never get here. We need to show atheistic and agnostic young people that our "faith" doesn't take away from their nontheistic life stance. Rather, it adds love, purpose, and community to it. At its best,

Unitarian Universalism can offer them an opportunity to live an authentic, whole-person life.

—◄o►—

JOHN B. HOOPER *is a retired research scientist, past president of the Unitarian Universalist Humanist Association, and a member of the boards of directors of the American Humanist Association, the Humanist Institute, and the Institute for Humanist Studies.*

The Importance of Science

David E. Schafer

One day, late in 1953, I received a phone call from someone on behalf of the First Unitarian Society of Minneapolis (FUS), the "Flagship of Religious Humanism," inviting me to chair the Music Committee. I had heard of the high quality of the music program, which included a chamber orchestra and a chorus led by the conductor of the St. Paul Civic Opera. I accepted the invitation on the spot; my wife, June, and I joined the society and never looked back.

The minister of FUS, Carl Storm, was a fountain of Humanist narratives, though he didn't call them that. I first heard him deliver a lecture on January 2, 1954. He spoke about Benjamin Franklin, and the lecture exploded my illusions that I knew something about the subject. When he spoke on John Scarne, the "world's foremost gambling authority," I felt that he could see a Humanist story in the life of any human being. This idea—the Humanist side of everyone—is still part of my concept of a Humanist narrative. What matters is the speaker's point of view. Storm's point of view was down-to-earth, and the content of his talks was significant and fascinating.

It seemed everyone who heard Storm's sermons admired them. In his book *Counselor: A Life at the Edge of History*, Ted Sorenson, John F. Kennedy's closest adviser, remembered Storm at All Souls Unitarian Church in Lincoln, Nebraska, as

> a dynamic young minister from New England, who preached every Sunday a brilliant and informative sermon. . . . He could expose hypocrisy in both public and religious matters more incisively than anyone I have heard or read since. His sermons drew me to regular church attendance in my teens. Unitarianism became a major influence on my life. . . . I even considered, briefly, a career as a Unitarian minister.

I felt the same way. I have never before or since belonged to a congregation quite like FUS. Years later, in my current Unitarian Universalist congregation, the Unitarian Society of New Haven, FUS has inspired me. I chaired the summer worship committee for ten years and led many of the services myself. Probably my favorite service, with a sermon titled "How I Wonder What You Are," compared Hubble photographs of the stars with the stages of an embryo's development. The Unitarian Society of New Haven chorus has sung many of my Humanist compositions.

Humanism and Science

A familiar Humanist slogan proclaims "reason and compassion," and both of these qualities are truly important—but they are not sufficient. Nothing is more essential to a definition of Humanism (religious, secular, or both) than the scientific worldview—not just the methods of science, but the results as well. Until the beginnings of the scientific worldview, genuine Humanism was impossible, because everybody, without exception, was completely ignorant of the basic facts about the universe and human nature.

Our forebears were all working in the dark. Reason is an important component of science, but it is not the same thing. The pre-Socratic philosophers were perfectly capable of reasoning 2,500 years ago, but they mostly got the facts wrong. What was missing until quite recently was a way to observe and measure and then to analyze and interpret the observations. In the immortal words of Dr. Seuss in *The Cat in the Hat*, "but you have to know how." To know how to explain, predict, and appropriately harness our environment and ourselves, we need a highly reliable way of ascertaining the truths about the world.

In his essay "Science and the Search for Meaning," UUA President Peter Morales suggests that science serves as a path to a free and responsible search for truth and meaning—in accord with the fourth Principle of Unitarian Universalism. In addition, Christopher Butler, in his book *Postmodernism*, maintains that the postmodern distaste for science amounts to a mindless and dangerous rejection of one of humanity's greatest gifts. So, to "reason and compassion" we must add "science."

A Humanist Narrative

Every religion, every movement, needs a narrative to give it meaning. What is our narrative today? What is life? What is a person? How did we get that way?

In our time, there can be only one integral narrative for humanity, the story built on the scientific worldview. Very briefly, it goes like this: The most recent estimates of the age of the universe put it at 13.8 billion years old. In three minutes of cooling after the Big Bang, the nuclei of hydrogen and helium stabilized. After about 400,000 years of cooling, the full hydrogen and helium atoms were stabilized. After a billion years—as a result of further cooling, condensation, and reheating caused by gravitational forces—clouds of hydrogen and helium atoms began to form protostars, and nuclear reactions began in the cores of these stars, forming all the heavier elements.

Some 9 billion years after the Big Bang, our solar system formed from the gravitational collapse of a giant interstellar molecular cloud. We know this because the oldest known meteorites in our solar system are roughly 5 billion years old, and our own planet is 4.6 billion years old. We do not know precisely how or when life originated on Earth, but the earliest physical evidence of life here is biogenic graphite from rocks 3.7 billion years old. Although oxygen constitutes 47 percent of Earth's crust, life then was anaerobic, since almost all oxygen was chemically bound. Then, roughly 2.45 billion years ago, small amounts of molecular oxygen began to be released into Earth's atmosphere, on account of photosynthesis by cyanobacteria. Slowly, over the next billion years, atmospheric oxygen levels rose to their current level of 21 percent. What keeps that level constant is not understood, but without it, the evolution of multicellular animals would at best have been severely limited.

Multicellular animals are best understood as elaborate cell colonies; larger animals such as human beings have circulatory systems that move molecules like oxygen and hormones efficiently and nervous systems that help cells communicate with each other quickly. The evolution of such complex organisms has naturally been slow. The genus *Homo*, to which we humans belong, appeared 2.8 million years ago, and our own species, *Homo sapiens*, is a mere 160,000 years old.

From this perspective, we humans are complex machines, huge colonies of living cells, each cell in turn made of chemical elements whose atoms originated in stars. The elements that compose our magnificent brains, with their incredible neuronal networks enabling consciousness and storing fantastic memories, are "star-stuff," as millions of people have heard Carl Sagan say. His point has now been made even more emphatically—"We are not figuratively but literally stardust"—by his popular successor, Neil deGrasse Tyson.

This story of cosmic and biological evolution provides the foundation of the Humanist worldview that includes awe and wonder at the incredible nature of life. And Humanists feel a sense of meaning and purpose from participating in the ongoing psycho-cultural evolution that is our human responsibility.

◄●►

DAVID E. SCHAFER *is past president of the Unitarian Universalist Humanist Association and a retired physiologist. An accomplished musician, he has composed hymns and choral music using Humanist texts.*

THE LIGHT OF MY LIFE AND THE FIRE IN MY SOUL

MICHAEL WERNER

For all the talk about reason and science, Humanism is really about a passionate love affair. It is a love affair with life, not a mythical hereafter. Humanism is a love affair with a progressive vision of civilization in which each of us can add to our growing library of wisdom, our evolving knowledge of what there is and what is truly important. None of the great achievements in history would have been possible without a love of the adventure of learning and the adventure of creating a better life. Our great cultural achievements in science, art, music, literature, philosophy, history, psychology, and political thought all inform each other and have been born of that long Humanist tradition.

Both secular and religious people today have retreated from grander ideas to mere personal, inward meanings and purposes. The Enlightenment, modernism, and a commitment to progress have been challenged by the horrors of the Holocaust and occasions when reason turned against itself as a tool for power and control. We fear grand narratives, labels, and larger stories of how life is and could be. We live in a cynical, narcissistic age without vision, and our retreat from community and larger commitments has sapped our passions.

For centuries, Humanists have overcome huge barriers and thus made a real difference. They would never have succeeded except for their passion for truth, justice, mercy, and making the world somehow a little bit better.

Humanism is merely the ongoing, evolving life-stance that challenges us beyond atheism, beyond our own self-centeredness, and beyond our own fear of larger commitments to embrace the best of what we and society can be. The statement of our vision, the Humanist Manifesto III, is not a rigid doctrinal statement, but an evolving consensus. Its purpose is to help people understand what you can believe if you don't believe in God. It is merely a jumping-off point for the real ongoing quest.

Some have neglected to use the full breadth of Humanism's resources. Some people believe that science answers everything we need to know, but this viewpoint ignores the many tools the humanities have given us. Democracy and the concepts of human rights are gifts of history and civilization. Philosophy gives us tools for critical thinking and a conceptual framework. Literature and art heighten our awareness about what values are important. As Curtis Reece, one if the founders of modern-day Humanism, said in his sermon "The Faith of Humanism," we must relate to others purposefully to "weave the best personal values into a noble social order."

We human beings seek a whole, integrated story for our lives—something that gives us power and meaning, hope, joy, and purpose. This deep identification of shared values of all people is what Humanism offers beyond atheism. Most of us privately long for something worthy of our noblest devotion. Paul Kurtz wrote *The Transcendental Temptation* as a warning about the temptation of irrational, otherworldly visions, but his whole life reflected a Promethean urge toward a transcendent Humanist vision of how we might structure our lives in a profoundly meaningful way.

In our troubled anti-foundational times, it's time to take another look beyond society's failings, the universe's inherent meaninglessness, our own needs, and our avoidance of grand purposes. Instead, we should once again make commitments of the heart to pursue the best of who we and society can be. Being a Humanist takes passion, courage, and commitment. It requires a love of life that can help us rise above our age's vacuous, cynical malaise and empower us with a vision of what a Humanistic society can look like.

Humanism is a grander vision of life. It is a devotion to humanity and the biosphere that humanity is part of. It is our passionate commitment to the best ideals that are supported by what experience, science, and civilization have taught us. Humanism is larger than any of us. We have a duty to continue Humanism's evolving tradition, which

has inspired countless individuals to make the world better. At the same time, it motivates us to fill our lives with
transcendent purpose for a meaningful, exuberant existence
that makes life worth living.

―◦―

MICHAEL WERNER *is a past president of the American
Humanist Association and the author of* Regaining Balance:
The Evolution of the UUA. *He has been an active Unitarian
Universalist layperson for many years.*

Is, Ought, and the Other

David Breeden

"All by nature desire to know." That is the first sentence of Aristotle's *Metaphysics*.

Aristotle goes on to ask, What is the nature of existence? Is there meaning to existence? And does existence have an essence, despite the constant change in our world?

According to all the evidence we have found so far, human beings long assumed that the universe was chaos. The Greek word *khaos* means "a vast chasm." Various foundational myths from all over the world describe gods harnessing this chaos. And so those gods must be obeyed and appeased to keep the chaos at bay.

The Greeks appear to have been among the first to see that our reality is not in fact chaos at all but the most amazing sort of order. Most likely this recognition evolved as many Greeks stopped believing in the foundational myths of their culture—the gods. The order the Greeks saw depended not on gods but on the structure of reality itself.

Aristotle was correct, at least in his initial assertion: All by nature desire to know. The question we all face is how far to allow our curiosity to take us.

I have wished to know. This is the desire that drove me to Humanism.

I found Humanism in a small Unitarian Universalist group while I was an undergraduate. I grew up in a rural area in southern Illinois, an impoverished farming region in the Ohio River Valley that was the birthplace of American evangelicalism. The varieties of evangelicalism —from "country" Methodist to "hard-shell Baptist" to Pentecostalism—were everywhere, from one-room churches to storefronts. It was the religion of my parents. My mother was illiterate; my father dropped out of school in the sixth grade.

I grew up with revivals and "singings." I saw people "slayed" in the spirit, dancing in the spirit, and speaking in tongues. I've seen the effects of the "Holy Ghost" descending on a congregation. I've seen exorcisms. I've seen the laying on of hands and healing.

Part of this tradition involves reading the Bible, which, according to the tradition, contains all the wisdom for living that we need. Bible reading is to be a daily practice. By the time I was twelve—the traditional age of accountability—I had read the Bible for myself, the King James version.

I began to see, however, that what I read in the Bible did not square with what I heard from the preachers. I bought the idea that the God of the Old Testament had been transformed by the experience of Jesus into a father of another sort. But wasn't it there in black-and-white that Jesus wanted deep political change? Radical love? I thought so.

I got no satisfactory answers to my questions. And so I stopped going to church the minute I left home, which was right after high school graduation. I have never looked back. There were, I should add, no liberal religious alternatives to be found at that time in the region where I lived.

My parents could not afford to help me go to college, and they had no idea what an education entailed, so they couldn't offer any help there. What they did offer was the example of their own lives: Get an education, or live in poverty and subservience for life.

So I went to community college, then the local university. There I studied literature and philosophy with the vague notion that I could perhaps become a high school teacher.

One day, my American literature professor, a Harvard-trained man teaching Wallace Stevens, said, "I'm an atheist, of course, but the Unitarians will be kind enough to bury me."

I had seen the term Unitarian over and over in the author biographies of my *Norton Anthology of American Literature*. I had wondered what made Unitarian synonymous with the work of Emerson and Thoreau and Melville. I had assumed that Unitarianism had died off, gone the way of tall black hats, large buckles, and blunderbusses. When I heard otherwise, I looked up Unitarian in the phone book and went to see for myself.

At the Unitarian Universalist fellowship, I found engaged people laughing, smiling, mocking, questioning —free people living freely in the world. These were not like the people I had grown up with.

I was hooked. That was 1978. And I have never looked back. Because I was good enough at school to be offered scholarships, I fell in love with the university world and kept going until I became a college professor. But as a graduate of state universities, I was severely limited in my teaching options.

At all the small colleges where I taught, I always joined the local lay-led Unitarian Universalist fellowship. This was my experience of Unitarian Universalism until I went to seminary, some thirty years later.

I was an English major in college. Then I received a master of fine arts in poetry. Then a PhD in creative writing and Old English literature. I'm no scientist, in other words. But I know enough to believe what scientists say. I live in poetry and literature. But I don't live in superstition. For me, mystery signifies that which is not known, not that which may be thought of in a foggy manner.

Just as I agree with Aristotle that all people are by nature curious, I agree with Socrates that an unexamined life is not worth living.

Clarity of insight is the gift that Humanism brings to Unitarian Universalism, a gift that makes the UU philosophy relevant in an increasingly post-theological, post-religious world. We desire to know; we desire to live free, examined lives; and we need community. These are the things UU Humanism can offer to the post-religious.

Late in his life, the philosopher Richard Rorty—a well-known atheist—was asked by an interviewer if he could define holy. Perhaps the interlocutor thought the aging and dying Rorty would be stumped by the question or would fall into some traditional language of reverence. But Rorty was not stumped by the question. He responded, "Holy: the hope that someday my remote descendants will live in a global civilization in which love is pretty much the only law."

For a Humanist, holy doesn't have to do with particular places, words, or books—or even particular ideas, which must always be under interrogation. Holy is a place where and when the basics of human flourishing are realized. Among these basics are the inherent worth and dignity of every person; a world community that stops the battling between clans, tribes, and nations; and respect for the planet and its creatures.

Humanism begins not from the assumption that there is no god but rather from the knowledge that no scripture or god concept adequately answers the questions Aristotle asks in his *Metaphysics*. In a 1917 lecture, sociologist Max Weber declared the world "disenchanted," meaning that the enchantment had all gone. The world, he said, is—thanks to science—no longer under a spell. This state of affairs did not make Weber hopeful, since he believed that science could supply only what Hume calls the *is*, but not the *ought*—that is, facts but not values. But too many people live still in Weber's confusion, a confusion that drives us back to old superstitions.

The *is* has become our *ought*, because we have done well at times in learning peaceful and fulfilling ways of being. We have sometimes included "the other"—encompassing all those we choose to place into other tribes—as worthy of flourishing. Painfully, slowly, perhaps we are learning peace. Anthropologist Robert Ardrey makes this point well in *African Genesis: A Personal Investigation into the Animal Origins and Nature of Man*: "We were born of risen apes, not fallen angels, and the apes were armed killers besides."

Ardrey characterizes our nature, our *is*, yet we also developed as social, communal animals capable of incorporating the other into our tribes. This *is* implies our *ought*, because our species by nature wants to grow and to know: That is how animals such as we humans became the animals we are. We want to know, and we do work to know, unless our birthright of free thought is wrenched from us by political repression, poverty, or other systems of oppression.

All by nature desire to know. We must strive for a world where all can know.

—◆—

DAVID BREEDEN *is senior minister of the First Unitarian Society of Minneapolis, president of the Unitarian Universalist Humanist Association, and a former college professor.*

NOTES IN THE MARGINS

JAMES C. KEY

Scanning the books of Papa's library, I couldn't help but notice the copious marginal notes in his prized book collections: the complete works of Shakespeare, American and English writers and poets, Latin and Greek texts, and more than a few King James versions of the Holy Bible. These scribbles often noted his suggestions for rewording for clarity, references to related texts and sources, and, not infrequently, disagreement with what the authors had to say. Many notes reflected his wry humor. As a bookworm in the public and school libraries, I knew better than to mark any book in any way. Even school-books in the early grades could not be marked, as they were on loan and had to be returned clean for the next class to use, or the offender would face a hefty fine. So it was shocking to an eight-year-old to notice these penciled notes in the fine books I knew my grandfather cherished.

Papa lived in North Carolina, and his eldest daughter, my mother, lived in Virginia about a hundred miles away. She was a single mother of five. After many extended absences, her husband, my father, had abandoned the family permanently before my birth. During school holidays, Mother would often take me on the Greyhound to see Mama and Papa and some of her eleven brothers and sisters whenever she hit a bad patch. My siblings were much older and seldom made those trips. So it was during those visits in my early years that I began to explore Papa's library—with his permission, of course. He tried to hide some of the more lurid True Detective magazines to which he subscribed, but I inevitably found them and was fascinated by those marginal notes as well—very educational for a young lad.

During those many visits, I was invisible to most of my uncles and aunts and older cousins. However, Papa was pleased with my curiosity and took an interest in my theological education. Over time, I came to realize that although he identified as a Social Gospel Methodist and was an enthusiastic advocate for the social justice element of that movement, he was highly critical of the Gospel element as he saw it being preached and practiced in the Jim Crow South.

He was a member of a large Methodist Episcopal Church South congregation and received the minister's visits with enthusiasm. They spoke regularly and with great intensity, with Papa challenging the theological justifications of church-supported segregation and other errors of theology he observed. He was highly critical of the absence of any prophetic voice by white clergy on the immorality of this social construct.

These conversations, debates really, were most informative for an inquisitive child who was always eavesdropping. They always left me with questions that my Methodist catechism teacher was unable to answer: Why would a benevolent God condemn people to hell? Why would a loving God not allow certain types of people into heaven? How could you reasonably explain three gods in one? It just didn't make sense to me.

And those notes in the margins always intrigued me! On every visit I found an excuse to browse Papa's library to look for and try to understand his marginal musings. They provided great insight into his self-education in Latin and Greek, with particular emphasis on translations of the Gospels in the Christian Bible.

On one of those visits, I was browsing an old, worn, zippered Bible when my eyes stopped at a bold inscription in the margin of one of the Gospels: "Bull Shit!" I laughed loudly, which alerted Papa to my snooping. It launched a long conversation between a curious kid and a delighted-to-influence grandfather. He explained the importance of reason as I matured and developed my own understanding of God and the universe. He told me about the Jefferson Bible, the document that Thomas Jefferson created to clarify Jesus' teachings to provide "the most sublime and benevo-

lent code of morals which has ever been offered to man."
Jefferson omitted anything that was "contrary to reason,"
deleting anything that could not be supported or verified.
Papa introduced me to Jefferson's deism and the notion of
a benign "watchmaker" divinity.

Throughout that visit, he valued my doubts and welcomed my questions. Months later, my mother and I moved
to North Carolina to live with my grandparents for what
turned out to be two years. That move initiated a two-year
tutelage by my grandfather in the application of reason to
all things I found curious. The experience set the stage for
my early embrace of Universalism and, later, Unitarianism,
in belief if not in membership. I remained active in liberal
Protestantism as I grew older, married, and started a family, all the while a cultural Christian and moving toward a
belief I would ultimately identify as religious Humanism.

Like the proverbial frog in the hot oil, I tolerated the
increasing discomfort of the theology of liberal Protestant
communities as I moved the family around the United
States. Living and working in Asia increased my multicul-
tural interactions among people with different theological
and philosophical worldviews.

After living all over the United States and Asia, I moved
to a small town in coastal South Carolina and was finally
introduced to Unitarian Universalism . . . by a Presbyterian
minister! The minister thought I would be welcomed by
some folks who were organizing an emerging Unitarian
Universalist congregation. She was right. The frog had

become uncomfortable enough in the hot oil to jump out and become a part of a religious community that welcomed doubt, reason, science, and intuition more than certainty.

Not long after joining this Unitarian Universalist community, I was diagnosed with stage IV non-small-cell lung cancer and proscribed a palliative treatment of chemotherapy that ultimately lasted ten months. The prognosis was grim: Mortality rates were 95 percent within one year and 99 percent within five years.

In hindsight, I realize I moved through the five stages of grief quickly. I sped through denial. I had, after all, smoked as an adolescent. But I quickly entered the angry stage. I had quit smoking more than thirty-three years before the diagnosis and had eaten properly, exercised regularly, and seen my health-care providers as suggested. I shouldn't be facing this diagnosis! I have no recollection of the bargaining stage. As a religious Humanist, I believed that my recovery was entirely dependent on the effectiveness of the available science, my own positive attitude, and the visualization techniques I had been introduced to at Duke University Hospital. So there was no bargaining and no depression, the fourth stage of grief. As I reached acceptance, it became clear to me that it was precisely my emergent Humanist belief that equipped me to face what then seemed like a death sentence.

There was no deity to blame or petition for a cure, no miracle hoped for. There was, however, a revelation, if you will, that this newly acknowledged Humanist life view liberated me so that I could choose a path that put me in control of my treatment and recovery. It was this belief system that led to healing.

My realization of Humanism as a healing point of view led me to look back at my financially strapped, single-parent household. Despite the hard times, frequent bean dinners, many moves, and rude questions from adults, I never felt that our situation was my fault. It wasn't some sin, original or recent, that had led to our lifestyle. Nor was it because of some God that someone had made angry. Papa's insistence on applying reason to all challenges spiritual, moral, and ethical gave me the insights that led me to Humanism: first to my Universalist views that rejected the notions of sin and hell, and then to my Humanist views within Unitarianism that embraced the rational and the inherent worth and dignity of humankind.

As I researched the disease, consulted with medical professionals, underwent treatment, and relied on the support of my faith community, I became increasingly convinced that human energy and understanding would get me through the nightmare. Great science from a world-class medical university, compassionate care from a legion of health-care professionals, a loving embrace from my faith community, and a positive outlook of hope all contributed to a full recovery and excellent health fifteen years on.

I believe that my commitment to religious Humanism within Unitarian Universalism saved my life. I had a grandfather who encouraged me to examine all things good and bad through a lens of reason, including reading, study, research, considering alternatives, and honoring intuition. I had a community of heretics who supported me with compassion, encouraged my approach to restoring health, and never judged. And I had a family who was there at every step and never suggested I needed to get right with any Divine. All of this and more continue to affirm and strengthen my identity as a religious Humanist.

—◂○▸—

JAMES C. (JIM) KEY *is the moderator of the Unitarian Universalist Association and its chief governance officer. He is a member of the Unitarian Universalist Fellowship of Beaufort, South Carolina.*

HUMANISM
IS ABOUT
HOW WE LIVE

BEYOND THE OLD PARADIGM

AMANDA K. POPPEI

When I went for Candidating Week—that all-important weeklong event when a prospective new minister meets the congregation she hopes to serve—the committee that selected me hid my search packet. It was just too dangerous to let the secret out.

A little background: I am a third-generation Unitarian Universalist (UU), raised in the 1980s and 1990s at the First Unitarian Universalist Society of Albany, a beautiful New England–style meetinghouse with a Humanist-leaning congregation. I had planned on ordained ministry since the eighth grade, after a really good Rite of Passage year. After a move to Washington, D.C., where I attended All Souls Church, Unitarian, I enrolled at Wesley Theological Seminary, a Methodist school. I wanted to get out of the Unitarian Universalist bubble where I'd spent most of my life and to gain a stronger footing in the Christian stories that I really hadn't heard growing up. What I had heard—often and insistently—was conversation about the Humanist–theist divide, about those who did and those who didn't believe. Raised in a staunchly Humanist household, I could have been knocked over with the proverbial feather the first time I heard my childhood minister tell me that she thought there must be something bigger than herself out there. How . . . not UU, I thought.

My understanding of Unitarian Universalism, though, expanded as I attended different congregations in college and, of course, at All Souls, with its High Church feel, a choir that wasn't afraid to sing gospel songs, and a minister who preached about the importance of Jesus. By the time I graduated from Wesley Seminary, I was comfortable with all kinds of language and metaphor, and I would have told you that the best part about being UU was that you could take a spiritual journey while remaining at home in Unitarian Universalism—that the movement was broad enough and deep enough for all our words, all our beliefs. For myself, I found the richness of God imagery appealing (and, to be truthful, I enjoyed the sense of mild rebellion from my Humanist upbringing), and so I chose the theist end of the debate.

Now, as I headed into the search for my first settled congregation, I had completed the form that the Search Committee had given me. I had begun the description of the spirituality section with the comment "I am a theist, through and through."

Which was precisely what the Search Committee now needed to cover up. You see, I was the candidate at the

Washington Ethical Society. These societies share many of the values of Unitarian Universalist congregations, but they come from a different movement and history: Ethical Culture, founded in 1876 by Felix Adler, focused on ethics and put deed before creed. Throughout the twentieth century, as Unitarian Universalism explored Humanism, Ethical Culture found itself more firmly within the Humanist sphere. In fact, some Ethical Societies added Humanist to their name for extra clarity, like the Ethical Humanist Society of Philadelphia. A few theists attend Ethical Societies, but the majority of members would describe themselves as agnostics, atheists, and Humanists, or simply Ethical Culturists, preferring to focus on the positive description of ethical engagement rather than the negating term of atheism. Technically, Ethical Culture is considered a non-theistic tradition: Like some forms of Buddhism and other Eastern traditions, it simply doesn't concern itself with metaphysical questions. Those are left up to the individual to contemplate personally, while the community comes together around shared values, its work for justice in the world, and a commitment to ethical living in relationship.

So there I was, the new candidate for the senior leader position at the Washington Ethical Society, and the committee that found me couldn't even display my search packet because it contained that dreaded T word, a description of personal belief that was at best irrelevant to them and at worst off-putting. I approached the week with a mixture of excitement and worry. Could I respond to questions with both integrity and reassurance? Would the Ethical Society members find me acceptable, even if they knew about my spiritual journey? And—most importantly—could I even lead a Humanist congregation when I wouldn't describe myself that way?

Well, they did end up asking me to be their senior leader, and I've never misrepresented myself to my congregants. When they ask specifically, I tell them that I find personally meaningful a wider range of language and metaphor than that which I use publicly as their leader (the Ethical Culture equivalent of minister). Some of them attended my ordination as a Unitarian Universalist minister, where they saw a little bit of that wider range in action, and others are happy just to know that I understand and respect Ethical Culture's unique language and heritage. But the biggest journey is not the one that the congregation took in welcoming me (or in joining the Unitarian Universalist Association, which this particular Ethical Society did just a few months before they asked me to be senior leader) but the continuation of my own spiritual pilgrimmage.

These days, I am proud to call myself a Humanist. And really, I have the Ethical Society to thank for that.

As I mentioned, growing up as a Unitarian Universalist, I thought that Humanists were the opposite of theists, two ends of a seesaw. There's even a catchy little satirical tune, set to the melody of "You Are Sixteen Going on Seventeen": "I'm a theist, you're a Humanist, we are both UU." I knew that there was room in Unitarian Universalism for theists and Humanists both, but when I was younger I assumed that you had to choose between them. My journey as a teenager and young adult went back and forth on the see-saw, trying on different ways of being, different languages, different ideas. And so my early claim to theism meant, of course, that I couldn't also be a Humanist . . . right? I had made my choice, and while I reserved the right to change my mind, I certainly didn't want to be too wishy-washy on such an important idea.

Then came my leadership at the Ethical Society and a resulting exploration—for my public role, but also for my own understanding, my own experience of personal integrity—of what Humanism really meant. In the early years, I would refer to my congregants as Humanists with a careful little wording trick so as to not entirely include me in their number. But in researching Humanism for an adult education class that explored the idea of Human-ism in different world religions, I had my "aha" moment. I managed to teach not just the students but also myself that Humanism was much broader, much bigger than the box I had tried to put it in when I was a youth. Far from being the end of the seesaw, the polar opposite of theism, Humanism was really an attitude about life, about the human experience. Yes, Humanism has historically been grounded in a naturalistic metaphysic, but that's not the important part. Humanism, I came to realize, is primarily about who we are connected to, what we think about each other, and how we work for justice in the world.

These days, I describe Humanism as a broad set of ideas, a movement that spans centuries and religions (I credit Alan Bullock's classic *The Humanist Tradition in the West* for some of that thinking and my Ethical Culture mentor, Leader Richard Kiniry, for introducing me to the book). No matter what else they believe, Humanists insist on the inherent worth of every person. According to Humanists, we are all part of one human family and are connected to the rest of the natural world—part of a cosmic story far bigger than we can imagine. Humanists believe that we're in that story together and that our work is to write our chapter with as much love and dignity as we can. In the Humanist view, change will happen in our world because we make it happen, and the change will take all of us.

I loved growing up Unitarian Universalist. I'm honored to serve our movement as a minister, even as my bi-denominational self crosses borders to the Ethical Culture movement, whose distinct heritage and identity hold history and promise. And I still believe that you can take all kinds of spiritual journeys and remain at home within Unitarian Universalism's broad embrace. But I'm no longer interested in perpetuating the old paradigm of the Humanist–theist divide. I never have liked polarities and dualities; they lead to all kinds of misconceptions, and this one is no exception. The Humanists are old and stuffy and intellectual, one stereotype goes. They prefer debates to emotion, and they don't like to sing—really, they're practically secularists, and who even knows why they go to church. The theists are leading us down a path toward evangelical Christianity, says another stereotype, and all they care about is sneaking prayer into every service. If they have their way, there soon won't be any difference between us and the Presbyterians. Polarities breed stereotypes, and stereotypes are always oversimplified, often wrong, and usually pretty boring.

On a practical level, the stereotypes and, more importantly, the whole idea of a Humanist–theist polarity, keeps UUs squabbling with each other rather than focusing on the real needs and challenges of the world. It holds us back, ironically, from living out the full promise of Humanism: to honor both the real and important diversity and the deep unity of the human family and to create a world where that whole family flourishes. What if, instead of imagining Humanism as one end of a seesaw, we saw it as a possibility that is open to all, regardless of their metaphysical beliefs? That's the lived reality of "deed before creed," the organizing idea behind Ethical Culture—and, as it happens, behind Unitarianism, too: In 1866, James Freeman Clarke, Unitarian minister and early organizer of the American Unitarian Association, wrote: "We think it possible to have a Church, and even a denomination, organized, not on a creed, but on a purpose of working together. Suppose that the condition of membership was the desire and intention of getting good and doing good."

Unitarian Universalism always has and always will have a beautiful tapestry of beliefs represented within its fold.

Over the years, I have found both joy and solace in the words and images from our Christian heritage, and even more from the works of Henry Nelson Wieman and other process theologians who expanded the concept of God and invited us into a sense of connection with the ultimate. I'm proud of, and grateful for, our theological ancestors and those who continue the work. But from its conception onward, Unitarian Universalism will always have at its core an engagement with this world—including its wonder and challenges—and with the human experience and the human promise. Thus, Unitarian Universalism is essentially a Humanistic religion, in the broad and embracing sense of the word *Humanism*—which is the sense I like best, anyway.

Serving as I do now a congregation that embraces this broad Humanism and concerns itself little with the metaphysical, I can see the possibility in this focus. I'm proud of the Washington Ethical Society's long history of justice work, the members' continued commitment to a world that is different, and their clarity that changing the world is up to them and others who share their passion. The members of the society take the idea of deed before creed to heart, trying hard to understand those who believe differently than they do on any number of religious or political levels. As a religious movement, Ethical Culture is grounded in ethics found in relationships. One of our catchphrases is that we work to "elicit the best in others and thereby in ourselves." Members of the society regularly wonder aloud how they can elicit the best in a friend, a co-worker, or even someone working on the other side of an issue. For these Ethical Culturists, Humanism is a deeply lived tradition and has nothing to do with being nontheist (though Humanists might also be that). It has to do with being human and with being human together. Humanism ultimately arises from, and is a response to, our shared experience as human beings in this world, at this time.

This kind of Humanism—that's what I believe in now. I'm a theist every other Thursday afternoon—that is, I still appreciate God imagery and language, although the question of belief in God no longer feels like the most important one to me. Perhaps I'm a reverentialist: someone who searches for and celebrates the experience of reverence, however it comes. My metaphysical grounding is essentially naturalistic (that is, I don't believe in an omniscient, omnipotent being that acts in the world outside natural law), although I am firmly convinced that there are mysteries we don't understand.

The most important, or perhaps just the most beautiful, theological idea to me is grace. In more traditional religious frameworks, grace has a clear definition—in our progressive tradition, grace, like most theological concepts, has a broader definition. Unitarian Universalist minister Fredric John Muir, in *Heretics' Faith: Vocabulary for Religious Liberals*, calls it "a consciousness of unity, a sense of divine order, a listening to life." Grace is connected to the traditional idea of freely given blessing—it is every unexpected beauty and possibility that unfolds in life. Sometimes that grace is an accident of nature, the sunset on the long drive home; sometimes we offer it to each other, as in the care shown in a time of loss. Sometimes I glimpse a power of love behind that grace, moving it into our lives; sometimes it seems that grace just appears, a part of the world around us, the way the sidewalk sparkles after a rainstorm. There is perhaps a seesaw in my life, a traveling back and forth among more and less theistic ideas and images. But at all of the points, I see now, I am also a Humanist.

And this is the belief that I'll carry with me and that is woven through all of Unitarian Universalism: the broad, generous Humanism that is about our connection with each other and our love of the world and that gets right off the seesaw and welcomes everyone to play.

◄o►

AMANDA K. POPPEI *is the leader of the Washington Ethical Society and an ordained Unitarian Universalist minister.*

MYSTICAL HUMANISM

DAVID BUMBAUGH

I suppose I was a Humanist before I ever heard the word or had any understanding of its meaning. Indeed, for most of my career, I resisted the label, feeling that labels inevitably limit possibilities. However, late in my career, discovering that those who knew me best had determined I was a Humanist, I quietly accepted the designation.

Ironically, my Humanism is rooted in what I would define as a deep mystical experience. I was not yet sixteen years old when my world changed, time replaced eternity, and I was driven from my garden of innocence forever.

It happened one afternoon in 1952. School had ended for the day. I was walking down the familiar street that took me from the town's only high school to my after-school job in a small grocery store. Neatly piled in two equal stacks, my schoolbooks were lying on a notebook that made a familiar pressure against my left wrist and the top of my hip. My schoolmates poured along the same street, in clots of two or three or more, laughing, shouting, calling to each other, or engaged in private, intense conversation, apparently unmindful of the life that flowed through them. I walked alone, observing the interactions, not part of them except as the observer is always part of the observed—not lonely, but conscious of being alone.

Both sides of the street were lined with trees—maples and oaks, brilliant in their fall colors. In the crisp, clear autumn air, they looked almost incandescent. The street gutters lay ankle-deep in fallen leaves. When you stepped through them, they gave off a dusty, musky odor that seemed the very essence of dried sunshine. On the west side of North Potomac Street, the mansions of the wealthy sat like smug dowagers on the crest of a small ridge, separated from the commerce of the street by vast expanses of green lawn, neatly raked, with only a vagrant leaf to punctuate their immaculate surfaces.

Darting between automobiles, I crossed to the west side of the street, just below the point where Oak Hill Avenue and North Potomac Street intersect. I stood looking south down the steep hill that poured traffic past city hall and into the public square. Everywhere, the world was alive; wherever I looked, there was a vibrancy, a joyous fullness of being that no words could ever adequately express. I could see it in the flow of traffic, in the stir of leaves, in the exuberance of my schoolmates; I could feel it pulsing in my veins; all was in rhythm, each thing resonating with every other thing. I stood for the briefest of moments, entranced by a sense of the absolute rightness and perfection of that instant. It was then, in the midst of that moment of perfect joy, that I suddenly understood that I must die. Neither I, nor this place, nor this moment could escape the remorseless flow of time and death. That experience entered my soul as a thousand others like it had not, precisely because, for the first time, I confronted the passingness of things, the precious quality of all that is unique and finite and never to be repeated. Tinged with melancholy, that last moment of innocence has remained with me through all the years that have passed, and in the autumn, every flaming tree reminds me of the perfection of every moment and the oblivion into which it and we must pass.

Death had brushed me long before I encountered it on that autumn afternoon. My mother died when I was nine months old. In some corner of my mind, there persists a hazy, unconnected memory—almost incoherent, perhaps created rather than remembered—a memory of me as an infant, being held in strong arms, staring into an open grave. There is, somewhere, near the center of my being, a great cry of protest, a wail of anguish and outrage at being abandoned and forever closed out—a cry that was never made, a protest for which there were no words, a grief that had no concept to give it form or substance. It is still there—the unformed memory and the unvoiced cry—tinting my life with melancholy, making me always, in some final sense, a loner, driving me to sympathy with those whose lives are lived on the margins, defined by the shadows of existence. Almost from the very beginning, my life had been marked by death, and that early wounding, though never healed, became a source of whatever drive or skill or insight or sensitivity I developed.

And of course, there had been other deaths. Death was no stranger in my world, but until that beautiful afternoon, death had remained an abstraction. It was something that had happened, would happen again, but did not involve me personally. Somehow, I had never made room in my life for death. Like many young people, I had assumed that while everything around me changed and death struck here and there, I and rest of the world of which I was the center would, in some crazy way—perhaps because I had been inoculated so early—prove immune to the ancient curse. That was the garden of innocence from which I was expelled one sunny October afternoon. There, on that busy, public street, while the world hurried by on nameless, routine errands, I came face-to-face not with death, but with my death. My world lurched out of its orbit of perfection and has never been the same again.

I remember that I was not frightened. Nor was I angry at the thought that I must die. Rather, I was deeply saddened. In that moment, I recognized that because of death, the world must forever remain a mystery. No matter how long I might live, the world would be forever in process; there would always be something more to learn, some book unread, some possibility unexplored. History would be forever incomplete, with no knowledge of the ultimate consequences of actions or decisions. No matter what experience I might amass, what insight I might acquire, what memories I might squirrel away against the coming winter, all must evaporate and dissipate at the moment of my death. My piling up of fact upon fact, my search for knowledge, my love of life, and my thirst for justice were no more permanent than the structure of blocks a small child builds in a busy doorway.

Curiously, despite my early, deep, and persistent religious indoctrination, it never occurred to me then to seek refuge in familiar, orthodox religious doctrines about life after death, the resurrection of the body, or any other such promises that death might be defeated. And yet, in some strange way, that moment of confrontation on the streets of my hometown one beautiful autumn afternoon confirmed my longtime drift toward a career in the church. The confrontation with my death posed a challenge that I accepted almost without knowing: to discover, if I could, the various faces of death and to seek to understand its relation to life; to explore the construction of meaning in a universe that, for all intents and purposes, seemed indifferent to the hopes and schemes of the human community; to relate the human venture to the larger enterprise of life on this planet. In many ways, that has been the focus of my ministry for more than half a century.

Many assert that Humanists have been shaped by unresolved anger and hurt resulting from early encounters with traditional religion. Others suggest that Humanists have thought their way to a rejection of conventional religious expression by subordinating their feelings to rationality. Both of these assertions carry an unspoken judgment that Humanism is a brittle, immature stance that healthy people eventually outgrow. That has not been my experience.

I grew up in a deeply religious family. But our faith did not grow out of or receive much thoughtful exploration. My early religious experience was in the Salvation Army, a fundamentalist, evangelical faith, and was occasionally supplemented by doses of Pentecostal worship services. In my family, faith was to be felt and accepted, not weighed, measured, or otherwise thought about. Somehow, all unaware, I grew out of that religious context. It was not so much a conscious rejection or a consequence of anger or disappointment; nor did I think my way clear. At some point, the religion of my childhood simply became irrelevant.

When I was preparing for college—the first in my family of origin to take that plunge—my uncle, who was my surrogate father, took me aside to warn me that in college I would encounter skeptics and unbelievers who would seek to undermine my religious convictions. I would need to be on guard against the blandishments of false friends and a culture that looked on religion with contempt. I listened to him respectfully while realizing that his warning had come too late. The faith he wanted me to protect had already evaporated.

Curiously, despite that recognition, I entered college with the intention to prepare for ministry. My call to ministry had little to do with a desire to help others. Nor was it focused on a need to proclaim some great truth. Rather, I was driven by a need to explore and understand the world that opened for me that October day in 1952. While in college, I worked part time in a factory that made trim for automobiles. The mind-numbing experience of the punch press and the insistent demands of the press line reinforced my need to seek some structure of greatness beyond simple survival. A ministry vocation might allow me to wrestle with ultimate concerns.

In that sense, my ministry was always about under-standing the world, our place in it, and the construction of meaning in human lives. I had no time for unresolved anger or for nursing ancient hurts or resuscitating dead gods. I was fascinated by the recognition that in as far as we know, human beings are the meaning-bearing, meaning-creating instruments of a universe that, apart from us, seems to have neither meaning nor purpose. There grew in me a convic-tion that because we are instruments of meaning in this universe, it matters what kind of meaning we build with our lives. Not knowing why it matters, or to whom or to what, I was certain that in every decision, we create the person we will be and subtly change the universe, however minutely, forever. Gradually, as astute parishioners would later proclaim, I became a mystical atheist.

My response to the world was never scholarly, but it was intellectual. I sought insight from a wide range of scientific and philosophic sources. But I did not think my way into my peculiar form of Humanism. My ministry was a constant attempt to find the language that would help me speak about my early mystical experience with rich emotional valence—something I would later call a language of reverence. I wrote and rewrote hymns and readings and liturgical resources. I stubbornly refused to use language that suggested a range of beliefs or convictions I could not fully embrace.

My mysticism was anchored in a profound appreciation for the natural world, an unshakable conviction that we are rooted in unbreakable coexistence with all that is, that the distinctions we make between ourselves and others, between human and nonhuman, between living and non-living are useful fictions but that beneath those distinctions is a bond that unites us with all that is or was or ever shall be. Therefore, the choices we make, the work we do, and the lives we construct echo throughout time and space.

I preached this conviction for fifty years. If it is true that preachers only ever have one sermon, this was mine. More importantly, this conviction shaped my response to the moral challenges of the times. At eighteen, I was confronted by the demand that I register for the draft. The question before me was, Who do I become as a consequence of the decision I now make? Offered an exemption because I was a college student preparing for ministry, I rejected it and asked for classification as a conscientious objector. Later, when responding to issues of racism, classism, and other social injustices, I was driven by the same question. Who do I become, what meaning am I creating, if I enter into this struggle or choose to stand aside? Almost without exception, I chose to enter the struggle. And the same question shaped my personal life—in the family, in the congregation, among colleagues, and in friendships: In this response, what meaning am I incarnating, what witness am I bearing, what person am I becoming?

This singular focus resulted in my often being out of step with others. I was rarely willing to put the purported interests of institutions or conventions ahead of my own need for integrity. Whether in the parish, or among colleagues, or in the seminary, I often said no when others wanted me to say yes. Though it may have seemed otherwise to those I frustrated, I was driven not by a desire to be contrary, but by a need to be true to my own sense of integrity.

Now, in my twilight years, humanity has entered a time when the naturalistic mysticism I preached so consistently over my career is harder to sustain. The world of nature that seemed so alive and vibrant all those years ago now seems threatened and damaged perhaps irrevocably. Anyone who understands the serious nature of the multiple crises confronting the earth and its children must acknowledge that though life and the planet may survive the catastrophic consequences of our thoughtlessness, it is no exaggeration to acknowledge that the world as we have known it is coming to an end.

Humanism, lacking any supernatural referent, must find a new voice, a less optimistic vision; it must sing its song in a minor key to a generation that is facing an end time of our own devising. The Humanism that will speak to our current condition must be more humble, more compassionate, and less certain and self-assured than it has often been. It will be humbled by the reality of a world threatened not so much by superstition or irrationality, despite the noise that sometimes fills the airways, but by a cascade of unintended consequences flowing from an all too-frequently arrogant assumption that the world is ours to shape by rational efforts into the blessed community. Without abandoning reason as we face the great disruption of our time, today's Humanism must embrace the conviction that the world is not only stranger than we know but also stranger than we can know. We live within limits and must respect those limits. To borrow a concept from the late Henry Nelson Wieman, Humanism, to be a useful response, must learn to "live richly with dark realities."

Ironically, in this time of the great disruption, I find myself faced with the same challenge that confronted me all those long years ago. Knowing that all things pass, realizing that death is the price we pay for having lived, understanding that we cannot know the final outcome of all our living and doing, how are we to confront the end times? And the answer is still the same: Day by day, moment by moment, infuse your life with meaning, shape the person you want to be, love this evanescent world that is the context of our existence, and leave to the unknown that which cannot be known.

—◄○►—

DAVID BUMBAUGH *has served Unitarian Universalist congregations in Alexandria, Virginia, and Summit, New Jersey,
and recently retired as professor of worship and preaching at
Meadville Lombard Theological School in Chicago. He is the
author of two books,* Unitarian Universalism: A Narrative History *and* The Education of God, *as well as numerous articles.*

EMBRACING A LIVED HUMANISM

MARK WARD

I didn't have the word for it at the time, but what I've come to know as Humanism was at the center of my religious orientation—indeed, I would say my religious faith—from as early as I can remember. It wasn't something I had thought out; it was something I felt. I knew it when I had the deepest sense of being at home—at home in the natural world, at home among people I loved, at home in work and play that fed me and stirred my imagination, at home in it all.

David Ignatow writes of this connectedness in his poem "In No Way": "I am of the family of the universe, and with all of us together I do not fear being alone." My faith is centered in the conviction that there is ultimately no separation between me, us, and all that is. This conviction is not only a source of comfort but also a source of power. It guides me when I am dispirited or confused, when I am tempted by hubris or idolatry. As a faith, it locates all value in what is, not what is supposed. It grounds me, and it stirs my imagination and my hope.

My faith had its origins in the reforested lots near the suburban tract home where I grew up. I wandered around those woods, exploring creeks and digging under rocks. It was there that I learned a deep affinity for the natural world—a love that I have never lost. But that was only the beginning. My true religious awakening came at the church of my childhood, the Unitarian Church of Princeton, New Jersey (now the "Unitarian Universalist Congregation of Princeton"). It was a booming church in a booming time—the early 1960s—and my family was swept up into the middle of it.

My memory of religious education is something like a continuing panorama of all the astonishing ways that we humans over the ages have imagined our place in the universe: everything from tales of the Bushmen to Jesus, the Carpenter's Son. I was not guided to any particular beliefs. Instead, my time at church was imbued with a spirit of discovery and the adult leaders' implied trust that I could find my way to a meaningful and ethically centered life. In a sense, my religious education married my sense of wonder with the joy of being part of a caring community—a community where I knew I belonged, where I mattered, where we all mattered.

All this, as I say, was impressionistic: a matter of feeling more than thinking. As I grew, I also experienced some of the quirkiness of religion—the clay feet, as it were, of our movement, which, despite its aspirations, can be reactive, elitist, and blinkered. So, heading off to college and young adulthood, I drifted away.

But life, in time, would pull me back, and in returning, I came to examine my early religious leanings. I gravitated to a sort of religious Humanism as a place to camp out and review the landscape. The notion of God had never resonated with me. The arguments for God's existence that I came across as a philosophy major I found unpersuasive, and the guilt-inducing sermons insisting I turn to God seemed tedious. Religion, it seemed, was not a source of revealed mysteries, absolute truth, or absolute anything. It was a way that we humans had devised to make sense of the world and our place in it. And so the Humanist idea that our chief work as religious people is to celebrate the world in which we live and aspire to ethical living made sense.

Heading into seminary, I explored and was intrigued by the rich history of Humanist thought and its emergence in our movement, from John Dietrich and Curtis Reese to our role in the first Humanist Manifesto and Kenneth Patton and the Charles Street Meeting House. But as I read Humanist writers, something niggled at me, too—something that smacked of aridity and arrogance. The Humanist dedication to reason in religion seemed admirable, but I came to wonder, Is that all there is? David Bumbaugh addresses this question in his 2003 essay "Is There a Humanist Vocabulary of Reverence?" (in *A Language of Reverence*, edited by Dean Grodzins): "We must have the ability to speak with power about what is deepest and dearest, about the focus of our ultimate commitment, about the source of human good, about what is so precious to us that we cannot betray it without losing our souls."

Reason is an important tool, sure—an essential arbiter of truth claims about the world. But religion is grounded someplace deeper, where we experience the joy of living and are connected intimately with all that is. Religion is an entirely human experience but one that we get in touch with using some pathway other than intellectual argument. In religion, we seek to address not just what is but also what we hope for and what we dedicate ourselves to. We rely on it to navigate the shoals of love and grief, compassion and estrangement, gratitude and disappointment, and mystery and wonder.

As Bumbaugh suggests, religion deserves reverence; it requires a vocabulary and a theology. This theology demands no intervention of unearthly forces but invites us to open ourselves to different ways of living and learning. It considers "the human" a niche in the vast, intertwined plenitude of being. And just what is our niche? We are fragile, fallible sorts for whom just being is a blessing and love is a polestar.

To be honest, when asked about my religious orientation these days, I equivocate. I haven't abandoned Humanism, but I wonder if it's enough. If religious Humanism is to be more than a historical artifact of our movement, then it must grow and, like all living things, evolve. One direction that this evolution needs to take is a larger sense of the human. There is more for us to glory in than just "the wonder of our thought," as Malvina Reynolds put it in the hymn of my childhood "O What a Piece of Work We Are." More remarkable is our capacity for compassion—how we can see ourselves in others and accept a larger duty than serving our own needs. More than anything, the work of religion, of tying us back to a source of meaning that we can trust, is centered on this sometimes-elusive capacity. The transformative power to love is the saving grace of our species. How might Humanism more deeply embrace this human capacity as central to our religious nature?

This larger perspective also opens us to wonder and the kinds of global experiences where language fails us. Ralph Waldo Emerson famously wrote of how once on a walk he suddenly felt "glad to the brink of fear," an experience where it seemed "all mean egotism" vanished and he seemed to become "a transparent eyeball" floating in "the currents of the Universal Being." Whatever we may think of Emerson's metaphor, that sort of transcendent experience is something we all know. We affirm it as the first source for our "living tradition."

These experiences are transcendent not because they carry our gaze outside the realm of the natural world. But they offer a dimension of, or a perspective on, the world—a perspective that is greater than our own. In that way, transcendent experiences both inspire and humble us. They show us the limits of our knowledge while also reminding us of the astonishing beauty and complexity of the world around us. As Bumbaugh puts it in the same 2003 essay, they show that we are "children of a universe that is not only stranger than we know but stranger than we can know."

There is more than enough in all of this to inform a Humanism concerned with not just the intellectual plane but the dailiness of life, the struggles we endure trying to make sense of our lives, not to speak of this resplendent world into which we are thrown. Laid out before us is the long tapestry of a human striving to know, love, and find meaning in our lives and the world about us. Our brief lives give us time only to snatch a glimpse of what our place might be amid all this.

How will we find peace and serenity? How will we awaken to whom we are meant to be, to our true duties in this life? How will we approach the deep truths of existence? We will use what we have been given. What we have to work with is simply the human—all that which our clever minds and yearning hearts can muster.

And maybe it is enough—enough to cultivate a fitting gratitude for life and love, in which we are attentive to each other and a universe that sometimes inspires and sometimes befuddles us, at home in it all.

─◦─

MARK WARD *is the senior minister of the Unitarian Universalist Church of Asheville, North Carolina.*

LOVE AS THE ETHICAL BASIS

GINGER LUKE

I grew up in the sand hills of Nebraska. The land has gently flowing hills. When I looked out over the hills with the wind blowing across the grass, it seemed quite similar to watching the Atlantic waves rolling in toward the beach. I often realize, when driving back to Nebraska after being away, that I breathe easier and slower again, not unlike when I look out at ocean waves.

I grew up close to the land. My father would take me for walks across the prairies and call out the names of the grasses like blue grama and sand bluestem. He would lean down, pick a blade, and chew on it. We spent hours working in the family garden, planting and harvesting peas, radishes, strawberries, green beans and wax beans, carrots, tomatoes, and potatoes. I remember picking the potato bugs off the potato plants. We hiked through the wild roses under the pines and oaks as we walked down to a little lake below our house, where we found pasqueflowers in the early spring, followed by wild asparagus and, later, the cattails and arrowhead rushes. The little lake (a pond, some called it) was fed by the Minnechaduza Creek, which flowed into the Niobrara River. We canoed on the Niobrara, above where it flowed into the Missouri.

I always knew I was part of that natural world. The idea that human beings and nature were two separate things would have perplexed me. The world was filled with mystery, but a mystery of which I was a part. You couldn't walk out of it, because you were in it and it in you.

There was great power for creation and destruction in the world I grew up in, but the power was not conscious, planning, or manipulating. This power invited exploration and discovery; it elicited awe as well as caution. And I was a part of it because I was a human being. Everyone else was a part of it, too.

And in that amazing sense of place, I experienced love. It was the ethical basis for the life of the people in my family. I was unconditionally loved. You know our human hard-wired trait of always reaching out to help someone if they are falling or tripping beside us? That's the world I grew up in. If you slipped, someone helped you. If something was heavy, people helped you carry it. We were a part of the natural world, and we respected that world and valued each other. And if that weren't so, as I looked out at the world, I knew it was because people were oblivious to their harmfulness or were hurt or afraid.

The love I experienced was created, given, and received by people. It shaped how I cared about people, helped them, yearned to learn more about those I had never known, and thought of those who came before me and would come after me. We were creating the best world we could, and our actions were motivated by our image of the world that might be. The world was in process, and our job was to participate the best way we could. (Yes, later I loved those process theologians.)

Years ago, I helped establish a Unitarian Universalist campus ministry at the University of Nebraska. The college students were amazingly motivated as they planned their entire program. Shortly after we began, a conservative Lutheran graduate student joined our group. I thought he was there to try to convert us, but as he kept coming, it seemed he was trying to figure us out. One day, he said to me, "I think I have figured it out. I think I understand you. You don't control your actions because God told you to. You do it because it is what you think is right." "You've got it," I said. The reason I don't kill is not that God told me not to kill. It's because I don't want a world in which people kill each other. I refrain from stealing, not because God told me not to but because I don't want to live in a world where people steal. I reject hate, not because God told me not to hate but because I don't want to live in a world filled with hatred. And I love and care for people, not because God told me to do so, but because that is the kind of world I want for myself and for those who come after me.

Humanist minister John Dietrich may have written it best in his 1934 pamphlet, "Humanism":

> If we live in a great impersonal universe with no friend to guide, it matters tremendously how we conduct ourselves for we are actually the makers of human destiny. We are not simply individuals who have a beginning in life and an ending. We are links in the endless chain of life. To us has been committed all that life has won from chaos in all the ages past. Only through us can that trust from the past be transmitted to the future.

My mother was the choir director in the Presbyterian Church. I had a pin with twelve bars attached for the twelve years of perfect attendance in the Presbyterian Sunday School. I believed that God is love. Often, I have said if people would just stop right there—that God is love—I would probably still call myself a theist, because to this day, I feel that the strongest power in this world is love. It brings me both great joy and, when it is absent or distorted, great pain. Love is what encourages creativity, empathy, beauty, peace, a sense of belonging, and comfort.

It was that same Presbyterian mother who, when she was ironing one day, said to me, "I think heaven and hell are what we create here on this earth." She doesn't remember saying it, but I do so remember hearing it.

When the natural world is cruel or vicious, it is love—human love—that holds and comforts me and gives me solid ground on which to stand. I have never thought what the insurance companies call "acts of God" were ever really acts of God. Who wants a God that causes or allows tornados, floods, or other natural disasters?

The Boy Scouts of America requires Eagle Scouts to believe in God. On several occasions, I, who call myself a mystical Humanist, have worked with young Unitarian Universalist Boy Scouts to try to find an understanding of God that they could honestly say they believed in, because truthfulness is another expectation of Eagle Scouts. We talked about being a tiny part of something so much bigger —the entire universe. We talked about the love between each other and family and even those we don't know, who have given us so much—not just the people, but also the essence of love itself. We explored the amazing mystery of life and death and the sheer excitement of learning. I encouraged them to ponder the moments when circumstances caused them to stop and just be present. We talked about what seems to hold us when we feel so alone. And we discovered how some people consider all these examples the presence of God or God itself. Could the boys honestly say they believed in these experiences? I have been proudly present at several Eagle Scout award ceremonies—knowing more than most how much deep reflection went into the final decision to accept the award.

When my brother died from cancer at age thirty-three, I remember driving down the highway thinking there must be lots of little gods—in that sunset, in that tree, in the snow on the ground. When my daughter died from cancer at thirty-four, I remember the incredible warmth from hundreds of people who sent their love, drew a picture, or said a prayer and whose hearts ached (physically ached) with mine. I know she lives to this day in me and in all those whose lives she touched. And that is everything.

And when human cruelty or violence causes pain and death, I look to human love, which I am not at all uncomfortable calling divine love, for comfort. I often find this love in my Unitarian Universalist community. The love within this community directs me to not just sit and take it, but to do all I can to stop the cruelty and violence. So experiencing catastrophe often causes me to act as well as to grieve.

Recently I walked across the Edmund Pettus Bridge to commemorate the fiftieth anniversary of the Civil Rights March in Selma, Alabama—a march for voting rights, for civil rights, and for respecting the inherent worth of everyone. My first husband marched across that bridge fifty years ago. He called himself an atheist. I would have called him a religious Humanist because he went down to Selma with his Unitarian Universalist minister. He was supported by a religious community in which he actively participated. He wasn't a Humanist outside of community. After he died, his religious UU community celebrated his life and acknowledged his gifts to the world at his memorial service. And today, as a religious community, our Unitarian Universalism knows that the religious work he was doing in Selma is not finished.

My current husband calls himself a Humanist—a Unitarian Universalist Humanist and an atheist. Even though he shakes his head when he sees a UU minister in a clerical collar and is disappointed at the renovation plans of the church building, he greets new people in the church foyer in a manner that they recall for years. He examines the building construction plans and helps plan the new heating and air-conditioning. He has led seventeen youth delegations to El Salvador. For years, he has rearranged the chairs and created the flyers for the Sunday forum. His work on immigration reform is known throughout the country. He is a leader in UU legislative ministry. He sells fair-trade coffee, tea, chocolate, and olive oil every Sunday. All of these are examples of what Dietrich means when he says, "It matters tremendously how we conduct ourselves for we are actually the makers of human destiny."

When I look at a sleeping baby or the wrinkled, arthritic hands of my mother; when I listen to Kiri te Kanawa singing the aria (cantelena) from *Bachianas Brasileiras* no. 5 by Heitor Villa-Lobos; and when my eleven-year-old grandson gives me a hug and says, "I love you, Grammie," I am stopped in my tracks at the wonder of life. The miracle, the science of cells and bodies, the unlikelihood that all of this could come together and create life itself, causes me to pause with great awe. And I am thankful. The medieval mystic Meister Eckhart was right: "If the only prayer you ever say in your entire life is thank you, it will be enough." I pray it often. I sing it, in Bruce Findlow's lyrics—"For all that is our life, we sing our thanks and praise." I live by nurturing and then passing on much of what I have received from life itself. My religious Humanism is filled with gratitude.

When I pray in public, I begin, "In the name of all that is sacred and holy." When I pray in private, I breathe and then I begin conversations in my head and heart with thanks for the giggle my granddaughter had as she tasted the cookies she just made and with thanks for the excited voice and running hug my grandson gave me as I walked into his house. I give thanks for the fragrant, pink and white blossoms of the magnolia blooming outside my window and for the voice of my ninety-one-year-old mother, who says, "I love you," as she hangs up the phone. My conversations continue into my longings to read more between the lines when my stepson talks to me about his mother; to use my resources, including money and time, more wisely; to better understand who I am and where I am going; to simply have fun—to live the joys of life; and, always, for less pain in the world.

Being a Humanist calls me to my better self. It holds me in blessed community during the good times and the hard times and allows me to continually search for more meaning and understanding in both the world of science and art. And my Humanism is shaped by love.

Participating in a religious community makes my Humanism whole because I don't exist in the world as a lone entity. I am a part of that whole; I knew this even as a child. Being a Humanist is a religious act for me.

May it always be so.

—<o>—

GINGER LUKE *is minister emerita of the River Road Unitarian Universalist Congregation of Bethesda, Maryland. She has also served as director of religious education at the Unitarian Church of Lincoln, Nebraska, and at the First Universalist Church of Minneapolis.*

Humanism
and Unitarian
Universalist
Diversity

Black Humanism's
Response to Suffering

Colin Bossen

Author's Note: This text was written as a sermon while I was serving the Unitarian Universalist Society of Cleveland. The congregation has a long history as a multiracial religious community. One of my commitments as the congregation's minister was to preach sermons that drew from theological traditions other my own. The essay is offered as an example of how a white anti-racist minister might use resources from the black Humanist tradition to help a broad spectrum of people make sense of one of the most perplexing and enduring pastoral and theological problems: theodicy.

We humans are naturally curious creatures. Confronted with the reality of suffering we want to know why we suffer. What, we wonder, is the reason for disasters like the earthquake in Haiti, Hurricane Katrina, or the tsunami that struck Indonesia?

Many people blame God, thinking that such calamities are, in the words of one minister in Haiti, "the will of God." It is easy to blame God. It allows an escape from human reality and responsibility. Suffering exists because that is the way God created the world. It is not something that we humans have much control over. If it is to be alleviated then we must turn to God to alleviate it.

Humanism offers a counter explanation. Instead of arguing that suffering is the product of some divine plan, Humanism posits that suffering has two sources: human action (either through folly or malice) and the randomness of nature. Under this scheme, it is not God who has the power to end suffering but humanity. True, humanity might not be able to eliminate all suffering, but humanity can at least limit much suffering.

So much of the pain that exists is of a human origin. Writing in the *New York Times* about the tragedy in Haiti, David Brooks said, "This is not a natural disaster story. This is a poverty story." Brooks notes that an earthquake of similar magnitude to that in Haiti struck the San Francisco Bay Area in 1989. In that instance only sixty-three people were killed. The final death toll in Haiti has not yet been calculated but will almost certainly exceed 200,000.

The difference between Haiti and the San Francisco Bay Area can be accounted in the vast disparity of wealth between the two locales. When the discrepancies are taken into account the reason for the current suffering in Haiti becomes clear. It is not "the will of God" as the pastor said.

It is the result of the very human decision not to share the world's resources and work to eliminate global poverty. This may be, in the pastor's words, because "human beings are too wicked" but if so it is not because that wickedness is punished by God. Blaming God for the situation lets human beings off the hook. It does not hold those responsible accountable for their actions and their failure to act. The tragedy is not a result of God's disapproval of human wickedness. It stems from the structural violence—the violence of poverty, racism, and economic colonialism—that comprises much of human wickedness.

Whether one places responsibility for suffering with God or with humanity is a theological issue. It belongs to the field of theology known as theodicy, which seeks to explain why suffering exists in the world. The African American and Unitarian Universalist theologian Rev. Dr. William R. Jones argues that everyone has a functional theodicy that "relates to his prevailing beliefs about the nature of ultimate reality and man" and that individuals make a fundamental judgment about the character of specific sufferings, whether they must endure that suffering or should annihilate it, and whether suffering can be eliminated or is an inevitable part of the human condition.

Exactly what your theodicy is has a lot to do with the overall shape of your theology. If you assign responsibility for suffering to God then you are almost certainly a theist. If you see suffering as redemptive in a cosmic sense then chances are you are some type of Christian. Most Humanists reject both these views and place responsibility for suffering squarely in the human realm.

Some Humanists even go so far as to argue that those who assign responsibility for suffering to God or declare that suffering is either redemptive or restorative are themselves involved in propagating further unnecessary suffering. Jones's *Is God a White Racist?* posits that suffering is not redemptive and that describing it as such makes the oppressed complicit in their own oppression. It is foundational for the development of black Humanist theology.

In Jones's view any form of Christianity that denies human responsibility for suffering or conceives of the pain of the oppressed as salvific is not Christianity at all. It is "Whiteanity—a religion of oppression." The antidote is not a more liberal form of Christianity or a Christianity that places priority on the needs of the oppressed. These theologies still do not place enough responsibility for ending suffering in human hands. Instead, the antidote is to pay special attention to the reasons for suffering and, if possible, to try to combat them. It is to embrace the Humanist position that something can be done about human suffering because so much of it is a human creation. Since, for people of color, a large portion of the suffering they experience is a result of society's racist structures, a special kind of Humanism is called for, one that takes into account the particular types of suffering the oppressed and marginalized experience. For Jones and some other African Americans this type of Humanism manifests itself as black Humanism.

Black Humanism is not just the Humanism of people who happen to be of African descent. It is a distinct theological tradition that emerged from the African-American experience. Anthony Pinn argues that it has five basic principles, some of which it shares with Humanism at large and some of which are unique. These principles are: "(1) understanding . . . humanity as fully . . . responsible for the human condition and the correction of humanity's plight; (2) suspicion toward or rejection of supernatural explanation and claims . . . ; (3) an appreciation for African-American cultural production and a perception of traditional forms of black religiosity as having cultural importance as opposed to any type of 'cosmic' authority; (4) a commitment to individual and societal transformation; (5) a controlled optimism that recognizes both human potential and human destructive activities."

Lewis McGee, one of the first African Americans to be ordained a Unitarian minister and founder of the Free Religious Fellowship, an intentionally interracial Unitarian religious community on Chicago's South Side, summarized his Humanist theology in these words: "We believe in the human capacity to solve individual and social problems and to make progress. We believe in a continuing search for truth and hence that life is an adventurous quest. . . . We believe in the creative imagination as a power in promoting the good life."

For Humanists, particularly for black Humanists, it is the creative imagination that provides hope to alleviate suffering. The "map to a new world is in the imagination, in what we see in our third eyes rather than in the desolation that surrounds us," writes Robin Kelly.

In the case of black Humanists it is the imaginations of, in Kelly's words, "aggrieved populations confronting systems of oppression" to which we should turn in seeking solutions to suffering. Since suffering in these communities is most pronounced, the logic goes, the solutions they have found and the visions that they have created are some of the most informative.

To offer an example, the maroon colonies served as havens for escaped slaves. They became places where the divisions of race found in the slave holding society were erased. Those of African descent mingled with the Native American population and distinctions between mulatto and recent African arrival disappeared. In these communities forms of African culture and religion, unrestrained by the brutality of slaveholders, re-emerged. Some maroon colonies lasted for decades, made alliances with local Native American tribes, and sued for peace with their white neighbors.

Black Humanism has provided me with inspiration. While I speak as an outsider I also speak with a deep appreciation for the forms of black Humanism I have encountered. A lover of techno and house music, I frequented dance parties in the electronic music scene in Detroit where social barriers between race and class often broke down. Music and dance created a space where social norms were ignored. Many of the artists involved in developing this music scene would not identify as black Humanists. Nonetheless, the black Humanist principles that Pinn describes were and are present in their work.

Alice Walker represents a form of black Humanism that might be more familiar than maroon colonies or underground dance parties. She writes, "I seem to have spent all of my life rebelling against the church or other people's interpretations of what religion is—the truth is probably that I don't believe there is a God. . . . Certainly I don't believe there is a God beyond nature. The world is God. Man is God. So is a leaf or a snake." Such sentiments are shared by many Unitarian Universalists. So too is Walker's emphasis on the possibility of human goodness as an antidote to the suffering we inflict upon each other. As she writes, "There is / indeed / a Buddha / in / every one / of us. / Loving humans / with all / our clear & / unmistakable / reluctance / to evolve / makes this hard / for most humans / to see."

The end to suffering, or the elimination of the suffering we humans inflict upon each other, may not be possible. But the dream of it, a dream found in liminal spaces and our human fellows, can spur us to action. It can cause us to accept responsibility, as we can, for the wrongs of the world and seek, somehow, to right them. When the paralysis of inaction or despair threatens us our imagination can provide the paths forward. This is the lesson I take from black Humanism.

—◄o►—

COLIN BOSSEN *is a Ph.D. candidate in American Studies at Harvard University, author of several articles, and co-author of two books. He served as minister of the Unitarian Universalist Society of Cleveland, Ohio, from 2007 to 2012.*

WHY UNITARIAN UNIVERSALISTS
NEED HUMANISTS,
AND VICE VERSA

PATRICIA MOHR

There are certain questions that I think Unitarian Universalism needs to address if it is to remain a viable religious
alternative in the twenty-first century. Starting with my own
history as a Unitarian Universalist, and continuing through
my evolution into a UU Humanist, I will try to describe
some of the struggles that people like me are experiencing
as they see changes taking place in the Unitarian Universalist Association—especially regarding its emphasis on
theological diversity and religious language. And then ask
the questions: Is there a place for Humanists in Unitarian
Universalism any longer? More importantly, why does it
need Humanism?

I have been a Unitarian Universalist for forty-three years,
since 1973. My story is similar to that of so many other
UUs: I left the Baptist religion in which I was raised soon

after I took a course on comparative religion in college and became interested in science, leading me to ask church leaders about science and religion. My questions were answered with the admonition to "just have faith." But the specific precipitating event for my leaving my childhood religion occurred during a meeting about missionaries. I asked why the church was telling us that if we didn't go over to "convert the heathens in Africa," their blood was on our hands. When I launched into an explanation of my most recent reading about the religions of different cultures, the leader of the group told me that my biggest problem was that I "read too much." This open example of anti-intellectualism was the nail in the coffin; I left that church and never looked back.

Later, my husband and I had children and began searching for a place where our moral guidelines would be reinforced. We joined the Unitarian Universalist congregation in Lincoln, Nebraska, in 1973, which had an agnostic Humanist minister and a predominantly Humanist congregation. In those busy years with two jobs and two young children, we never had the opportunity to attend the UUA General Assembly, so we assumed that our congregation was typical of all UU congregations. We quickly learned about the Christian history of Unitarian Universalism, but we never heard references to prayer, spirituality, or God in our Sunday services. Incidentally, this congregation still calls itself the Unitarian Church of Lincoln, not Unitarian Universalist.

Then, in 1986, we moved to the South, where I still reside, and joined the Unitarian Universalist congregation in Columbia, South Carolina. We became deeply involved in congregational leadership and active in district and national affairs, attending General Assemblies whenever possible. There in the early 2000s, we became aware of the push for more "language of reverence" using religious terminology (e.g., *faith*, *prayer*, and *god*) and to put a greater emphasis on, and to embrace, theological diversity. Unitarian Universalism was not just a religion anymore; it was a "faith." At this point, I decided I was no longer just a Unitarian Universalist; I was a UU Humanist.

Close examination of the history of Unitarian Universalism in the United States reveals that this tension between the more liberal, Humanistic UUs (in the U.S. Midwest and West) and the more traditional, theistic UUs (in the Northeast) began well over a half century ago although there were tensions going back to the nineteenth century. These differences are no longer so localized and appear to have now been submerged into the declaration of theological diversity. How can one not champion diversity? This is particularly true if one views another's theology as personal. It would be impolite to question it, much less debate or discuss it.

So where does this leave us with regard to our Sunday services? Should the minister pray or meditate? Should the minister mention God? Should the default theology be theism or Humanism? Our congregations have always had autonomy, able to determine their own governance with a free pulpit for the minister. However, I cannot remember a time when it was so difficult to distinguish Unitarian Universalists from members of other liberal religions. We "affirm and promote" the seven Principles and do a great deal of social justice. I would wager that the Methodist church in my city has similar values. In fact, the Methodist slogan is "open hearts, open minds."

Unitarian Universalism needs Humanists, atheists, and agnostics because this is the theological diversity that makes Unitarian Universalism unique. In particular, Humanists demand evidence for belief, and that evidence must be verifiable and reliable. Have our standards for truth changed, or is Unitarian Universalism just following the popular trend of using other epistemologies, with less reliance on rationality or reason?

These are my own personal perceptions, supported by conversations with many Unitarian Universalist Humanists and attendance at more than ten General Assemblies. Several worship services at these gatherings in the last three years were so theistic that I truly questioned whether I was at a General Assembly or the Southern Baptist Convention. In addition, we don't even sing songs from our primary hymnal, *Singing the Living Tradition*, very often anymore. Rather, one now hears songs in Spanish or African-American gospel songs or spirituals. In 2014 and 2015, the only song I recognized at the assembly was "Blue Boat Home"; I did not know any of the other songs. I appreciate and commend this effort to engage Hispanics and African

Americans, but I don't understand why we have to bring in theism to accomplish this goal.

My feelings may arise from the fact that I'm an older Humanist agnostic. I'm working to increase my tolerance for UU theism, but sometimes I feel as if I'm in a different religion from the one I joined in 1973. I thought I had joined a group of like-minded individuals, not an interfaith coalition that was working for common social-justice goals. While my own congregation now has an old-style (less theistic) interim minister, we had a Humanist minister for ten years, so I continue to be an active Unitarian Universalist. But what is the default theology for our ministers nationally? Should we alternate our gatherings, offering nontheism one Sunday and theism the next? Some large UU congregations have two services with different services (often in format and content). A small congregation like mine can't do this, so what should we ask of a new minister?

I'm equally concerned about the future of Humanism without Unitarian Universalism. If one defines religion as a specific worldview with rituals, practices, and an ongoing, lifelong caring community, then Humanism only qualifies in part. In fact, secular Humanists would disavow any connection to religion (even though the first Humanist Manifesto was presented as a religious document, signed by numerous Unitarian ministers). One of the issues Unitarian Universalism must always address is the Western definition of religion: belief in God. Many Eastern religions don't require belief in the supernatural.

Though it may seem strange coming from an agnostic, I believe that Humanism needs religion for its future just as much as Unitarian Universalism needs Humanism. Whether we consider community spiritual or not, almost all humans need a caring community for friendship, comfort, and support across the years. My congregation provides that sense of community for me, as well as the primary vehicle through which I work for social justice. There are several Humanist, agnostic, or freethinker groups in my city, but they do not offer this kind of continuing community. Having a critical mass in terms of number is another issue; it's difficult to build a group or accomplish much without sufficient numbers.

In summary, Unitarian Universalism needs Humanism because, as stated in our fifth Source, we must continue to refute "idolatries of the mind and spirit." We must continue to discuss and reevaluate the evidence we use when forming our opinions and beliefs. Not everyone will come to the same conclusions, but we will know why and where those beliefs come from. In addition, recent surveys reveal religious affiliation among young adults to be decreasing at a highter rate than among older adults. Consequently, the future of Unitarian Universalism may be determined by our ability to attract and retain people who question conventional religious ideas.

But Humanism needs Unitarian Universalism too. For those of us who need a caring community to share the joys and milestones and sorrows of our lives, a civic or social group will not suffice. I'm a Unitarian Universalist Humanist, and I hope to remain so for the rest of my life.

—◦—

PATRICIA MOHR *is a retired educator who has been a Unitarian Universalist and a Humanist for forty years. She has served in a variety of leadership positions in her Unitarian Universalist congregation and the Southeast District and as vice president of the Unitarian Universalist Humanist Association board.*

NONRELIGIOUS HUMANISM

MARIA GREENE

I am a relatively recent "convert" to Humanism and to Unitarian Universalism. Before that, I was a none, one of those who happily went along without religion in my life. Unitarian Universalism can fill the need for community and connection to a wider movement for people of all beliefs, especially for Humanists, who are cut off from most similar forms of community. But is there still room in Unitarian Universalism for a nonreligious expression of Humanism?

I lived within a few miles of my current church for twelve years with no idea that I would be welcome there. Greg Epstein's *Good Without God*, especially the final chapter, "Good Without God in Community: The Heart of Humanism," finally made the connection for me. Through my reading, I discovered that religion didn't always mean belief in the supernatural as I had assumed, given my conservative Roman Catholic upbringing, and I learned that a community close to me—the First Parish Church of Stow and Acton, Unitarian Universalist (in Massachusetts)—had a proud history of Humanism. But interestingly, I didn't learn this information from this nearby church very easily. When I looked closely at its website, I found plenty of Christian terminology (church, worship, minister, choir, hymns, religion, faith), but I had to look deeper to find this statement: "A belief in God is welcomed but not required within Unitarian Universalism."

Epstein's last chapter also included a call to get involved with a Humanist community, but this wasn't enough to get me through the door of a church. What finally got me out of my pajamas and out the door on Sunday mornings, like many people, were the needs of my growing children. Mine were approaching their teenage years, and I wanted them to experience church and have some education about religion, partly to inoculate them against the more virulent strains, I admit, but also to increase their cultural literacy. I also wanted to take advantage of the social and volunteering benefits of a church community that could involve the whole family. Learning about the human sexuality program at the church—Our Whole Lives—was icing on the cake.

When we did finally start attending Sunday worship services, I was surprised at how "churchy" they were. I could hardly tell the difference between the services and the Christian services I had attended in my life, except that Jesus and God weren't mentioned as often (and not invoked in the same way). Even the tunes of some of the hymns, accompanied by an organ, were the same as those

I remembered from my days singing in the choir at Mass; only many of the words had been changed.

When I mentioned my Humanism at coffee hour, I was met with polite smiles, an affirmation by the minister, and a quick change of subject—they were much more interested in my experience as a web developer and steered me over to talk to the communications committee chairperson. (I was happy to get involved, since that seemed like a good way to get to know people, and I still enjoy being part of that committee today.) I remember one friendly congregant telling me, "Most UUs don't care or know much about theology; we tend to focus on social justice." Humanism did come up in the "New-to-UU" class offered by the congregation, but other than that, I rarely saw or heard the word. I was surprised by this, and more than a little disappointed, but I was otherwise very happy with my new community. The members of the congregation had so much fun together, and I continue to be awed by their willingness to stand up for what is right and to do the hard work needed to make good things happen.

As it turned out, my little pocket of Unitarian Universalism surrounding progressive Boston has probably the most traditionally religious UU congregations out of all areas in the country. This eventually made sense to me when I learned of my own congregation's history. It began as the original Puritan meetinghouse that was established to meet the requirements for becoming a town back in the late 1600s. After much evolution, we certainly do not consider ourselves a Christian congregation today, but my minister is a lifelong Unitarian, educated at Harvard Divinity School (originally founded to train ministers for churches like mine), and the link to the association's Christian roots is strong and unbroken here. Like many UU churches, Buddhism has the second-greatest influence on the flavor of the congregation—an influence I have come to appreciate.

I learned from books and online research that other areas of the country, especially the Midwest, have more UU congregations that tilt toward Humanism, primarily as a result of the Fellowship Movement, which was used as a growth strategy there. I also learned that there had been some controversy surrounding the divide between Humanists and theists in the past that likely accounted for the mild discomfort I sensed but didn't understand when I brought up the topic at coffee hour

My online research also led me to the national Unitarian Universalist Humanist Association (UUHA). On its website, I found a full expression of the UU Humanism that I had been seeking. The site also celebrates the present and past role of Humanism in the Unitarian Universalist Association. And it provides a bridge between Unitarian Universalism and the American Humanist Association and the other parts of the organized secular movement that I was becoming increasingly involved with.

Eventually I became the executive director of the UUHA. Yet again, I found that my (and most people's) black-and-white assumptions about religion did not fit reality. I assumed that Humanists, as nontheists, would feel, like I did, that religious language, rituals, and symbols did not resonate with them and that the unqualified use of these elements in Unitarian Universalist spaces represented a disregard for the needs of UU Humanists. I learned from longtime Unitarian Universalists that most congregations and the national association itself had used less religious language in the past. Dean Grodzins, in *A Language of Reverence*, explains that the fairly recent call by former UUA president William Sinkford for a renewed "language of reverence" was enthusiastically taken up by many in the clergy. This call signaled to some the intent to elevate the importance of theism in Unitarian Universalism. Perhaps the black-and-white thinkers had deemed Humanism too intellectual, rationalistic, and cold and felt that some form of theism was needed to give the movement vitality again. For some, this theism included belief in an interventionist, personal God, while for others it was some form of pantheism, which identifies God with the forces and laws of the universe.

This issue wasn't simply the resurgence of the God-versus-no-God fight from the late nineteenth and early twentieth centuries. Instead, says William Murry in *Reason and Reverence: Religious Humanism for the 21st Century,* many Humanists agreed that Humanism had tended to overemphasize reason and underemphasize compassion and creativity. They saw religious words like *spiritual*, *faith*, *sacred*, *covenant*, *holy*, and even potentially *God* as redeemable and capable of being reimagined and redefined into a vocabulary that described something completely naturalistic but still religious and more emotionally satisfying than a purely secular vocabulary. The UUA latched on to the promise that this shared vocabulary, in which each listener could interpret the words in a way that matched his or her needs and beliefs, even if the person interpreted them differently, could solve the association's theological diversity problem. As UUA President Peter Morales put it in his essay "Belief Is the Enemy of Faith"—in which faith means our shared Unitarian Universalism rather than "belief without evidence"—we should downplay our differences of belief in the interest of intrafaith harmony. Most Unitarian Universalist insiders agree that this shared religious language helps in this effort and that it has become the norm in the denomination (see, for example, "The Emerging UU Consensus" by UU blogger and minister Tom Schade). The added benefit of a shared language is that it eases the way for interfaith cooperation, since it obscures our heresies from our traditionally religious partners who would be uneasy cooperating with atheists.

Where does this tacit agreement leave the UU Humanists, like me, who proudly consider ourselves nonreligious? Yes, Unitarian Universalism is a religion, declared officially so to the IRS, and religious Humanists emphatically don't mean religious in the sense of holding supernatural beliefs. Does my refusal to redefine religious, when applied to myself, demonstrate the narrow-mindedness and lack of imagination that nonreligious Humanists are now frequently accused of? I do not think so. It is the right of every Unitarian Universalist—theist or not—to self-identify however they would like and to have their perspective listened to and respected. I am more clearly understood when I use the most commonly accepted definitions of words and elaborate when I need to. But words have valence, to use the psychology term; they invoke certain positive or negative emotions in people, and personal experience is the main determinant of which emotions are triggered.

Those of us who choose to not redefine traditional religious words metaphorically are not rejecting wonder, awe, thankfulness, mystery, love, or any of those positive emotions. Nor are we rejecting being together in community and focusing on meaning, purpose, and being part of something bigger than ourselves. Instead, we find that religious words lead away from those states because of their valence for us. So where does that leave us nonreligious Humanists? Many of us are left outside Unitarian Universalism or physically present but increasingly frustrated by an unsupportive culture that does not acknowledge our perspective and instead blames us, as I have been told directly, for our "spiritual immaturity."

There are plenty of examples of lack of respect on both sides of this issue and still too much black-and-white thinking (including my own), implying that you have to push one side down to elevate the other. But this isn't the way it needs to remain. We can value all perspectives, theist and Humanist, religious and nonreligious, without conflating those two things and confusing the issue as we usually do. Belief is not the enemy, and we can value all perspectives by including all perspectives. We can encourage the formation of local groups around shared beliefs, not just Humanist, but also Buddhist, Pagan, Christian, and so on. We can encourage the exploration of belief and of combined religious identities—I personally know many Humanist Buddhists and even Humanist Pagans. My belief in Humanism is important to me, as others' beliefs are important to them, and I want it celebrated and included. I want my life to be enriched by a wide variety of other perspectives that I can engage with—sometimes critically, yes, but always with respect and love. I want my Unitarian Universalist congregation to be a microcosm of what I think we need in society.

We do not have to banish the use of traditional religious words to be inclusive, but we do need to consistently acknowledge those who do not use them. The UUHA provides a Freethinker-Friendly designation to congregations, based on their "What We Believe" statement. (For more on the UUHA's Freethinker-Friendly program, see the organization's website: huumanists.org.) For those looking to receive this designation I have been recommending one congregation's statement as a model: "Our community is made up of people who believe in God, people who don't, and people who are content to live with the mystery." This inclusive yet clear statement probably wouldn't even raise any eyebrows at the ministers' local interfaith clergy association.

Small semantic accommodations can be made to be more inclusive. For instance, we can refer to "Sunday services" instead of "worship services." During those services, we can ask people to "enter a time of prayer or contemplation," instead of just prayer. This kind of language is being used sometimes, but often it is not, because it is assumed that all are aware of, and in favor of, liberal interpretations of religious language. If members of the congregation felt that using traditional religious language was important to them, a service could start with a statement such as, "We welcome all religious perspectives, and none, and we ask the nonreligious to interpret any religious language metaphorically or poetically." Similarly, this could be included in the footer of any online message that needed it. That way, when a prayer begins with the words, "Spirit of Life, God of many names," the nonreligious Humanist listener could return the favor of accommodation and recognize that there was an effort made to include them. At this point, we need some sort of affirmative action—at General Assembly and in the pages of *UU World* magazine, for example—to show that the association is willing to include the nonreligious perspective.

There are many nonreligious community groups springing up nationally and internationally to fill the vacuum created (often unknowingly) by Unitarian Universalism. Most of them—notably, Sunday Assembly, Oasis, and university-connected communities such as Greg Epstein's Humanist Community at Harvard—welcome people with a range of personal beliefs, but the groups start from and maintain a nonreligious perspective and vocabulary. While Unitarian Universalism has been busy "getting religion," the trend in society is toward nonreligion. The trend is not necessarily toward atheism, although the way the poll phrases the questions and answers greatly influences the results. For example, a 2015 Pew Research Center survey called "America's Changing Religious Landscape" asked, "What are your religious beliefs?" Only about 3 percent of Americans chose the response "atheist." However, in a 2016 Gallop poll asking the same question, 11 percent chose the response "I do not believe in God" (and another 10 percent chose "Not sure about God"). The difference goes back to valence. The stigma associated with the word *atheist* is deeply embedded in our culture. Certainly, a large and growing segment of the population is nonreligious either in the sense of not believing in God (or not being sure) or in the sense of rejecting traditional organized religion. Many of these people are drawn to the new nonreligious communities for most of the reasons we are drawn to our Unitarian Universalist churches. They are similarly turned off from Unitarian Universalism because we only accommodate the religious style that they're unwilling to associate with.

I am seeking a community that accepts my family and me as our loving, positive, nonreligious, atheist, Humanist selves. If Unitarian Universalists decide that they now want to, as an association, only accommodate religious expressions of Humanism, this would be a personally disappointing but perfectly understandable thing to do. In an online chat conducted by the Church of the Larger Fellowship in 2015 titled "What We Share: UU-UCC Congregations," a theist Unitarian Universalist minister describes how freeing it is to serve a dual-affiliated Unitarian Universalist/ United Church of Christ congregation that is explicitly liberal Christian. Similarly, I have heard a UU Humanist minister, David Breeden, express how liberating it is to serve an explicitly Humanist congregation. Neither of them is unwelcoming to members with other beliefs, but both can point to the decision of the congregation itself to choose either a religious or a nonreligious style, thus avoiding criticism for not accommodating the other. Since we have congregational polity, this is perfectly fine. But we also have a national association with online outreach, a magazine, and a yearly General Assembly—all of which almost exclusively promote the religious perspective. This can make nonreligious Humanists feel unwelcome, no matter how much they love their local congregation or how sincerely the national leadership believes that it is being inclusive. It also means that we have unintentionally decided to turn away the majority of the growing population of nones.

One reason I love Unitarian Universalism is our values. I'm always proud of the times we score off the charts on the progressive side of any national poll question. I am also proud of our long history of Humanism—a history that none of the new models of Humanist community can claim. I value being open about my beliefs and being in community with and learning from people who are different from me. Most of all, I'm proud because of how Unitarian Universalists are generally on the front lines and show up and put in the time to translate our Humanistic values into action. I would like to be part of an association that is openly proud of its nonreligious members, clergy, and laity; does not require us to pretend to be something we are not in order to be accepted; and projects this acceptance throughout its outreach and other programs. The number of nonreligious Americans is growing steadily, and families like mine are seeking loving, deep community. Will we continue to let them walk by our doors unaware, or will we welcome them in?

—◦—

MARIA GREENE *is the executive director of the Unitarian Universalist Humanist Association and a professional web designer.*

Humanism and Social Activism

IT'S NOT ABOUT WHAT
WE BELIEVE OR DON'T BELIEVE

ROGER BREWIN

I came to both my Humanist and my Unitarian Universalist identities from origins not widely shared: birthright Humanism and social-justice Unitarianism. Most Humanists come to nontheism as young adults, losing their faith while in more traditional religions; I was raised in an atheist household, encouraged to judge all ideologies and theologies by the extent to which they made sense of the world and helped heal its hurts. I church-hopped out of curiosity and for friendship, but without religious conviction. My teenage support systems were mostly secular—Sea Explorers, various school clubs, and science-oriented programs. Free-ranging debate over the issues of the day, from civil rights to economic justice, were common dinner table fare in my socialist family.

At university, I discovered Student Religious Liberals, the Unitarian Universalist college community. We plunged into the antiwar movement and embraced the values of Woodstock Nation. We were naive, committed, and, amazingly, supported by the much older members of the sponsoring UU church. I did my first organizing there—helping end mandatory ROTC. I later entered UU campus ministry by way of skills (draft and pregnancy counseling) developed with the strong support of the Cincinnati cluster of UU congregations.

What attracted me to Unitarian Universalism was the widely shared notion that social activism is an integral part of a religious life (widely shared but, I discovered, less often put into practice). This conviction is central to my Humanism, which holds that life has no inherent purpose and that all meaning and direction must come from the efforts of individuals and communities to remake the world and our lives in it. Unfortunately, Humanism's beloved debates seldom give rise to the subsequent actions that would improve life. The comforts and practices of a liberal religious community, which we are moderately successful at creating, rarely impel action beyond our walls.

Both Humanist and Unitarian Universalist organizations frequently talk a better justice game than we play. Quick to respond to social-issue challenges with task forces, study resolutions, debate, and wordsmithing, we pour time and energy into mission statements and long-range plans, which frequently mention social-justice commitments, but less frequently fund them. In such documents, we honor our congregational covenant to promote the worth and dignity of every person, to respect the interdependence of all existence, and to live our UU Humanist values of reason, compassion, and community. All these commitments are welcome and needed anchors. Then, when we need to do the things called for by that covenant, such as show up at an immigration march or pay to install solar panels on our roofs, many of us hesitate.

Let me be fair: Some Unitarian Universalists and Humanists do walk the walk. There were large contingents of both groups at the New York City Climate Change rally in the fall of 2015, and the Moral Monday marches in Raleigh, North Carolina, earlier in the spring. Standing on the Side of Love, a UUA initiative, has inspired and coordinated a range of pro-immigrant and marriage-equality actions across the association; the emblematic yellow shirts and banners of that organization are ubiquitous. And the Black Lives Matter movement has galvanized many Unitarian Universalist clergy and activists to reach out in support of local African-American social justice efforts. Secular Humanist groups such as Center for Inquiry communities in Grand Rapids, Michigan, and Indianapolis, Indiana, cooperate with both nonreligious and interfaith area activists on a year-round service and social-action calendar. Their activities include Habitat for Humanity building projects and welcoming events for newly arrived refugees from the Middle East.

Of several UU Humanist social-justice projects, two in particular have had moderate success. Through our Banned Books project, initiated by the Justice General Assembly in Phoenix in 2012, more than four hundred copies of Hispanic-authored books, which had been removed from Arizona classrooms, were "smuggled" back into the state by individuals from more than a hundred congregations and Humanist groups. Ribbons Not Walls, a twenty-four-panel fabric arts display on immigrant experiences and culture, has toured more than sixty venues, including four General Assemblies. Utilizing the arts and creating partnerships with people outside the expected activist community, each of these projects involved numbers of people in fairly simple, direct action that can be replicated within local congregations or other groups.

Fifteen or so years ago, few Unitarian Universalist congregations had formal social-justice programming beyond study circles and educational programs. Humanist groups limited their activism to church–state separation and a few related issues. But Humanist ethics have influenced Unitarian Universalists for the better part of a century, and a social-justice consensus now replaces theological doctrine. More and more Unitarian Universalists will probably come to see activism as their primary "spiritual" practice. We UU Humanists should expect this of ourselves, as well as of our fellow liberal religionists. And our responses should move well beyond talking, well beyond intellectual assent.

Of course, talk is a wonderful and necessary prelude to action, but then we have to act! Getting a consensual statement of conviction makes us more effective—if in fact we then act. Who is more effective, twenty folks who have moved beyond the conversation and are sharing leaflets with the public, feeding and sheltering the hungry and homeless, mounting a picket line, or an entire membership debating and passing resolutions? Most of us are given to studying extensively and drafting consensus slowly, only to have those plans sit on the shelf while we return to the routine demands of congregational life or the upcoming calendar of events.

Consider the congregation that uses its prominent physical location in town to hold a monthly vigil to challenge police brutality. Or the Humanist group that moves beyond its monthly discussion of current events and begins registering voters or providing court watchers. Let them make those actions as much a priority as quality worship services or top-flight secular speakers. Let them provide the same financial resources for social justice as is given to pastoral care or music to enhance the monthly lecture. That's the heart of UU Humanism worth committing your life to.

Over the years, I have worked on behalf of First Amendment, immigrant, GBLT, and reproductive rights, and in the peace and environmental movements. That passion has centered my religious Humanism. Of course, not every Unitarian Universalist and Humanist will share this commitment, but they do need to claim our particular "costly heritage," to use Vincent Silliman's words in his hymn "Faith of the Larger Liberty," and together embrace the broad spectrum of progressive causes.

Both Humanists and Unitarian Universalists have experienced again and again the marginalization that comes with being on the leading edge of religious and social progress. We must stand with those who face such oppression. Given Unitarian Universalist history, we must be more than just another church with a slightly more liberal set of talking points. We must rally to the cause of science and reason and act when they inform us about clear challenges to human flourishing, be it climate degradation or discrimination against immigrants.

"Humanism has for me less to do with what we believe (or don't believe) than with what we do about what we believe." I spoke these words in accepting the UU Humanists' award for Religious Humanist of the Year in 2013. The same question applies to any claim of UU identity: What do you do that supports that claim? How do you take your convictions out into the world?

A Unitarian Universalist can be God-besotted or unapologetically naturalistic; a Humanist can be skeptical to the point of near nihilism or can embrace a wide and fuzzy range of practices of the human spirit. Our beliefs are all secondary: lived values in community, such as equality and resistance, do far more to show who we are. Assuming that a community is defined as exclusively Humanist or has the more varied makeup of many Unitarian Universalist congregations, I have only two questions: Am I welcome and respected as a Humanist, and are we going to be taking action together, as well as talking together and celebrating with one another?

How welcome are Humanists in the existing programs of Unitarian Universalist congregations?

- A group of Unitarian Universalists from a medium-sized church gathers weekly to study "sacred texts." The leader has previously introduced selected readings from holy books of various world religions. Tonight, each participant brought a book or written passage that has, at some point, "sustained or inspired" him or her. One person brings a collection of Buddhist writings; another, a volume of poetry. There are books by or about various contemporary religious, political, scientific, and ethical figures, and there is a Bible.

  We Humanists would love to study works of poetry and other literature with fellow Unitarian Universalists to enhance our aesthetic appreciation of life. We study works of science to add to our knowledge of how the world works. And we reflect on works of philosophy and ethics to improve how we relate to one another. Many of us Humanists enjoy reading scriptures of various traditions to gain an appreciation of the religious impulse and welcome the thoughts and opinions of our fellow UUs. These are all part of the "responsible search for truth and meaning," to use the phrase found on the frontispiece of the UUA's *Singing the Living Tradition*. But we'd like some recognition that the arguments ought to be logical as well as passionate and that evidence for truth claims ought to be prized. And Humanists like me would also be happy if one of the outcomes of such study was to encourage us to act ethically on the new self-awareness and knowledge we have gained.

- Some members of a Unitarian Universalist fellowship meet each Sunday before the service to discuss the previous week's sermon. Comments are supposed to be "carefully considered," and the questions should be "respectful." An informal code of conduct governs the discussion: Words such as nonsense (and anything else resembling aggressive disagreement) are gently frowned upon.

Now you would think Humanists would love this stuff, and indeed, when it is done well, this respectful approach to discussion is one of the aspects of congregational life that we appreciate. It is, after all, an updated version of the freewheeling Sunday service talk-back, a Humanist staple. But we Humanists often feel constrained by a very narrow view of what constitutes respectful disagreement and by the frequent assumption that Unitarian Universalists should never criticize any religious position or group.

Such a proscription is very new to our conversations and hard to justify. Our history is built on critical thought and its responsible expression.

Humanists wonder whether this Unitarian Universalist tradition of providing an honest critique of religion is fading. As Sophia Fahs writes in *Today's Children and Yesterday's Heritage*, "Some beliefs are divisive . . . some beliefs weaken a [person's] selfhood . . . some beliefs are rigid, like the body of death, impotent in a changing world." Some Unitarian Universalists suggest, in turn, that Humanists need to learn some manners. Can we not meet together in such discussions and find a middle ground—an open, vigorous, respectful discussion?

• A "spiritual practices" group is among several programs in a large Unitarian Universalist congregation. The agenda is eclectic: prayer, journaling, various forms of meditation and movement, chanting, and affirmation all take their place on the agenda. Members are encouraged to offer their own suggestions for practices that might interest others. Much of what is offered reflects what the congregation hears from the pulpit.

Most UU Humanists understand that such activities are part of how congregations serve the needs and desires of a wide range of members, from Western Buddhists to atheists, from liberal Christians to New Age seekers. But when spiritual themes seem to dominate both the programmatic life of the church and the Order of Service on Sunday mornings, we UU Humanists wonder how we fit in. Many of us do not object to spiritual content per se, but do lament that it often seems to crowd out other topics: naturalism, science-based themes, and ethical aspects of living. Other Humanists would like to see a broadening of acceptable practices to include dispassionate analysis and forceful argumentation. A diversity of approaches and content seems warranted by our diversity of UU perspectives.

Finally, I am not waxing nostalgic about the glory days of Humanist hegemony in our congregations. Here's what I remember: When I was new to Unitarian Universalism in the late 1960s, both Sunday mornings and weekday evenings in UU societies had a very different feel. This largely Humanist style had its faults. Our services could be overly intellectual and stiff; our programming valued erudition sometimes to the exclusion of opinion or passion. There was a fear of too much traditional religious language, but often there was nothing of great imagination to replace it. In some congregations, pastoral care could be scarce, overly analytical, and available only to the few strong enough to ask for it. We talked and debated at great length, but we were no more likely to act decisively on our conclusions than UUs are today.

As an activist, I am encouraged by the direction in which both organized Humanism and Unitarian Universalism are moving. There is still room for improvement; I look forward to these changes and will continue to advocate for them. As a Humanist, I still see a place for my religious approach within many UU congregations and, in some, a welcome for those new to nontheism. My calling is to live the core religious Humanist values of reason, compassion, and community and to recommend to my fellow UUs the tools of the wider Humanist movement. These tools include clarity of language; careful use of metaphor (the map is not the territory, and the symbol is not the reality); and the pragmatic, self-correcting methods of science, logic, and mathematics. I use and promote these tools not out of a conviction about their innate superiority but because they, along with other approaches, enrich our common journey.

—◄o►—

ROGER BREWIN *is editor of the journal* Religious Humanism *and minister emeritus of the First Unitarian Church of Hobart, Indiana.*

Being Human on a Warming Planet

Carol Hepokoski

My environmentalism and my Humanism are inextricably related. My Humanism tells me that human life is important and worthy of respect and care. My environmentalism tells me that to be human is to be part of an interdependent circle of all life; it is counterproductive to imagine ourselves as separate. My knowledge of today's world informs me that Planet Earth and, thus, human life are in danger because of the threat of global warming. I want to see life, including human life, preserved and thriving on our planet. My environmental Humanism compels me to work to reduce the causes of climate change—the human practices that threaten the survival of life on earth.

Religious Humanism: I have preached it, taught it, embraced it, argued with it, defined and redefined it, and tried to live it, for more than thirty years. So just what is religious Humanism, and what does it mean to practice it in today's world?

It is helpful to think of Humanism especially as we find it in Unitarian Universalism as a large umbrella that covers a wide range of understanding. Under the umbrella, we have all manner of atheists and agnostics, including Buddhist Humanists, Jewish Humanists, and Marxist Humanists. The umbrella holds spiritual Humanists and mystical atheists as well as those who consider these terms oxymorons. The umbrella shelters secular Humanists, who want little to do with a congregation (although this stance is an increasingly uncomfortable position for a Unitarian Universalist Humanist to hold). Some people seek shelter under Humanism from the fundamentalist-inspired God of terror, the "psychopath in the sky," as some describe this version of God. But among Humanists there are also Christian Humanists, who feel that God language and the Bible are too rich in human wisdom to be disregarded. They understand God as a metaphor for what is unnamable and unknown in the universe and for what is so much more powerful than we humans. I'm not one to kick out anyone who considers himself or herself sheltered under the Humanist aegis.

With such a wide range of sometimes-contradictory beliefs under the Humanism umbrella, what do we religious Humanists have in common? Most, but not all, religious Humanists have a preference for nontheistic language and a naturalistic, rather than a supernaturalistic, view of the universe. This is my minimalist definition of religious Humanism. We are more than nonbelievers, however.

Those of us who call ourselves religious Humanists have a strong reverence for life. Many of us experience a deep sense of awe before the mystery of life and death, those powers greater than ourselves. We share a respect for science and reason, and we are willing to live with ambiguity to live without definitive answers. We share a deep concern about injustice and the fate of human life, indeed, of all life on this planet, our home in the universe. We identify with the human story, even as we recognize it as intimately tied to the story of the rest of this world. Fortunately, there is a name and a tradition, religious Humanism, that describes what others may only call unbelief.

Some of the early Humanists were atheists, while others preferred to maintain a more openly agnostic stance regarding the supernatural. The focus of early Humanists, however, was not so much on questions of supernaturalism or even a critique of traditional religion, as is common among some forms of Humanism today. Their focus was on the human being, on human society and culture, on the possibilities of a better human existence, here on earth. Many early Humanists were committed to visions of a cooperative society, incorporating reason, scientific thinking, and a belief in evolution and progress. Humans are not perfect, but they are evolving. The arts were seen as glorious human achievements. Nature was seen as an important context of human life and a source of great inspiration. Indeed, these are important themes in today's Humanism as well.

One of the challenges for Humanism has been to become more inclusive, to see that the aegis of Humanism shelters a wider range of humanity. Some of the most interesting directions in contemporary Humanist scholarship are those opened by African Americans and feminists. These and other sources of our Humanist heritage are well mixed with the soil of movements for social change, especially the early labor movement in this country. This expanded territory opens up the question of social class and encourages religious Humanism to become more inclusive, which certainly is in line with its original aspirations.

Another challenge to religious Humanism came in the last quarter of the twentieth century, when feminists brought the consciousness of gender-inclusive language into religious discourse. We feminists pointed out that words like *man* and masculine pronouns in reference to human beings or to the divine were a reflection of a cultural bias toward men. The choice of language and imagery makes a difference in what is being communicated.

Another challenge to Humanism today is its potential to deteriorate into a dangerous form of speciesism. The charge is that the very word itself, Humanism, places human interests above the interests of other animals and living things and perpetuates the mindset that is responsible for our ecological mess. Instead of this anthropocentric view, critics advocate a biocentric view, where all life is deeply valued. While I appreciate this view and have advocated it myself in the past, I find it more intellectually and emotionally honest to acknowledge my human standpoint. After all, I am a human being, for better or for worse. And one of the things I like about religious Humanism is that it reminds me of who I am: a human animal, interconnected with the natural world. I have always understood that we are more and less than creatures governed primarily by reason and science. Our limited abilities to form just, peaceful, and loving relationships are a source of disappointment and challenge to us all. But where else, really, are we going to turn? What else, other than our human capacities, can help us find our way into the future on this dangerously warming planet?

Some years ago, I came across a painting that continues to inform my understanding of being human in the present time. *Cyborg*, a 1989 oil painting by Lynn Randolph, depicts a woman with a large, wild cat resting its head on the woman's head and its paws over her shoulders. The woman has her hands on computer keys, which are arranged in a keyboard fashion directly on the earth on a desert-like terrain. In the distance are mountains against a dark night sky punctuated with stars.

I have been captivated by the image in this painting for a long time because it suggests the ambiguous, dissolving boundaries of animal-human-machine. It reminds me that we humans are animals—that we come, literally, from animals. Animals are our ancestors, our relatives; we are kin. We humans are animal.

The image also suggests that all animals are now dependent on human beings for their survival. They rest on our shoulders. Our species has the power to disrupt habitats to such an extent that we hold power over animal life—indeed, over all life—on this earth. We may not like this power; we may understand it as morally wrong. But it is the case now.

Most liberal religionists agree that we humans, through the extension of our technology, have altered this planet and are responsible for the climate change that is affecting the life of all creatures on earth. It's easy enough now to look back and say that it was our hubris, our putting human wants and needs first, our idea that we are the apex of evolution, that created this mess. But it is both more and less complex than that: We humans are fallible. Sometimes our actions have unintended consequences. Who knew we were creating this potential holocaust for earth life? And by the time we knew, we were deeply embedded in the mess.

In the *Cyborg* painting, a woman of ambiguous ethnicity is interconnected with animals, machines, the earth, and the universe. The image helps show our being-in-the-world as human creatures today, and where we are going in the future. We have power, though it may be both more limited and greater than we realize. And we are responsible for what we have created intentionally or not. The painting also bears a message about the warmth and intelligence and connected-animal life that is on our shoulders. And the image might convey hope in the power of our minds, our technology, and our creativity—the power now at our fingertips in the complex, interwoven connection of human-animal-machine-earth that we have become.

I have called myself an environmentalist for nearly five decades now. Over that time, I have woven together an environmental philosophy and practice using pieces of wisdom I've garnered from others, as well as from my own attempts at living with more ecological integrity. I've been shaped by philosophies of simple living, bioregionalism, animal rights, deep ecology, sustainable agriculture, wilderness preservation, native habitat restoration, sustainable development, global environmental ethics, ecojustice, ecological feminism, and more.

From what I have learned, here is my best advice. Gravitate toward positive, life-giving approaches. Guilt and sacrifice are not effective motivators. Develop spiritual practices that nurture you and deepen your relationship with earth life. Consider what it means to be a good ecological citizen. Join with others to work together toward positive changes. Support an organization or two that work toward effective systemic change. Keep learning and observing, and know that we're in this for the long haul. Be ready to change your understandings as time goes on. Know that there is not one perfect answer that will provide the way out of this mess. Life in the future will deeply challenge our human flexibility and willingness to adapt. Consider what it means to live well. Build communities that work toward justice.

One of the environmental philosophies that I think might have special relevance for religious Humanists is environmental justice, or ecojustice. This perspective focuses on the effects of environmental degradation on human communities, especially on poor communities and communities of color. As the effects of climate change become stronger, we can expect those communities to be particularly affected (think, for instance, of the Ninth Ward in New Orleans after Hurricane Katrina). We can also expect that although coastal communities will be most affected by rising sea levels, poor communities there will have more difficulty navigating those impacts. We can also expect massive human migration, with all the social challenges this will bring.

I call myself an ecological or earth-centered religious Humanist. Taken together, these two terms describe my deepest commitments to human beings and to the earth. I am grateful for the sanctuary of the Humanist umbrella. And I am grateful that I am in a religious community, Unitarian Universalism, that welcomes, encourages, and challenges me to bring my values to life.

I have often talked with people who are just discovering religious Humanism, and it reminds me of the importance of this way of being religious. I remember again how crucial it is to speak about religious Humanism, to let those who are painfully questioning their religious beliefs know that they are not alone. Religious Humanists are familiar with the bumpy, sometimes lonely territory of "losing one's faith." We need to let others know that they can find a religious community where people who hold different, even heretical views, are appreciated and welcomed.

—◁o▷—

CAROL HEPOKOSKI *has served as the minister of the Unitarian Universalist Church of Rochester, Minnesota, and as a faculty member of Meadville Lombard Theological School.*

An Activist Humanist Life

Edd Doerr

Compassionate ethical naturalism: That's my bumper-sticker definition of Humanism, though of course, it's grossly oversimplified. I have been a Unitarian Universalist Humanist for the past sixty-five years or so.

Born the oldest of four sons into a caring, average, working-class Catholic family in 1930 in the Midwest, I grew up a rather typical Catholic—like most, I was not particularly devout, attending Catholic schools for eleven years. At sixteen, I started college after finishing high school in three years.

After a couple of years of college and stumbling across a copy of *The Humanist*, I realized that I was a Humanist. It's hard to say how I realized this, but it had something to do with going to a quietly secular, pluralistic public summer school and then university, plus reading science fiction since my first days in high school. In any event, the transition was rapid, smooth, and quite painless. I should add that relations with my family were unaffected. Many years ago, when I was a guest on a Boston television show, along with a Catholic monsignor, the host noted that I was a former Catholic and asked for comment. I said that some people are able to grow intellectually or spiritually within a single tradition, and some are not. The monsignor agreed, and that was that.

At about the age of nineteen, I began my lifelong career of writing from a Humanist point of view, beginning with letters to the editor. As one result, I received a letter one day from E. Burdette Backus, minister of All Souls Unitarian Church in Indianapolis. He commented on something I had published, and he invited me to visit All Souls. I did, felt that I belonged, and joined. Having sung in my father's Catholic church choir, I joined the All Souls choir in short order. I have now been continuously in Unitarian Universalist choirs for about sixty-five years, not to mention being a sometime Kol Nidre cantor for a Humanistic Jewish congregation.

I have been able to express my Humanist convictions in many ways. One way was to edit and publish a book in 1998 called *Timely and Timeless: The Wisdom of E. Burdette Backus*, an anthology of Backus's sermons and radio messages. (Backus, minister at All Souls from 1938 to 1955, was a signer of the 1933 Humanist Manifesto and the second president of the American Humanist Association.) But mostly I have expressed my Humanism through my professional work of writing, public speaking, radio and television talk shows, and other forms of activism and engagement, primarily on the subject of religious liberty. This work started with a position on the staff of Americans United for Separation of Church and State and led to my work as executive director of Americans for Religious Liberty for the last thirty-three years.

My publications include more than twenty books, contributions to at least twenty-five other books and encyclopedias, and literally thousands of columns, book reviews, articles, and letters in several hundred publications. My writing nearly always deals with issues of religious liberty, church-and-state separation, the defense of secular public schools, reproductive choice, women's rights, climate change, and human overpopulation, all of which I consider central Humanist concerns.

As a UU Humanist, I have been a delegate and workshop presenter on religious liberty issues at fifteen UUA General Assemblies and have been the Sunday morning speaker at more than a hundred Unitarian Universalist congregations in thirty-four states. I have also spoken to Ethical Societies and Humanistic Jewish congregations, not to mention Jewish, Baptist, Methodist, and Adventist congregations and uncounted university and other audiences. I wrote the 1982 UUA General Assembly resolution on religious liberty and church–state separation.

For many years, I have written a church–state column for *Free Inquiry* magazine. I was one of the original signers of Humanist Manifesto II and served as vice president and president of the American Humanist Association (AHA) for a total of fourteen years (six and eight years, respectively). During that time, I represented the association at international conferences in Norway, the Netherlands, Germany, Belgium, Spain, and Mexico, in addition to presiding at AHA conferences.

I also served for thirty years on the board of the Religious Coalition for Reproductive Choice, about twenty-five years on the board of the American Civil Liberties Union of Maryland, a short time on the board of the National Abortion Rights Action League, and some years on the board of the National Committee for Public Education and Religious Liberty.

I have been fortunate that my work has been tied closely to my UU Humanism. As a Humanist since about the age of nineteen and a Unitarian Universalist (back then just Unitarian) since about twenty or so, I am a Humanist UU or UU Humanist. I have always been aware of the diversity within both categories. I try to avoid arguments about whether Humanism is a religion, a term that is very hard to pin down. I like the term life stance and prefer never to define myself by what I do not believe, as that would be an endless list. I also place great store on this haiku that I wrote recently:

Labels may conceal

Far more than they might reveal.

They can mask what's real.

Further, nothing remains static; things evolve. In the late 1980s, for example, a UUA Commission on Appraisal study found that about 70 percent of Unitarian Universalists identified as Humanists. At about the same time, at a General Assembly at which I was a delegate, the delegates at the opening session were informally polled. The speaker asked how many of us were Christian UUs and about twenty-five people stood up. Jewish UUs? Another twenty-five or so. Muslim or Hindu? One each. Humanist UUs? A loud rustling of chairs as at least two-thirds of those present stood. This representation matched the Commission of Appraisal study. Most people I talk to agree with the perception that the percentage of Humanists in our movement has declined. Why? I cannot be sure. One hypothesis has to do with ministerial education. Many UU ministers receive their education in non-UU seminaries, where they are unlikely to have learned about Humanism. Some ministers have moved to the UUA from more traditional denominations and thus have little awareness of Humanism.

How does UU Humanism differ from secular Humanism? This seems to be mainly a matter of labeling, semantics, and style. There is great diversity within both camps. Some Humanists like and are comfortable with the organizational style of Unitarian Universalism, while others are not. Some in the latter group prefer smaller and less formal discussion groups, don't like to be associated with anything with a religious label, or have had a negative experience with a particular Unitarian Universalist congregation.

Humanism has historically shaped Unitarian Universalism. Half of the thirty-four signers of the 1933 Humanist Manifesto were Unitarian ministers. Then, in the decades after World War II, the growth spurt of Unitarianism was probably due largely to the growth of Unitarian Humanism. In the last two or three decades, Unitarian Universalist growth seems to have leveled off as Humanism seemed to cool in our congregations, though I do not know if the two trends are causally related.

UU Humanists around the country have told me that the most difficult thing about being a UU Humanist is that while the UUA readily acknowledges our inherent diversity, Humanists, like comic Rodney Dangerfield, "don't get no respect" in their congregations.

On the other hand, I have also heard that the most rewarding thing about being a UU Humanist is feeling at home in a respected national movement with a thousand congregations from coast to coast. These are anchored communities with buildings and ample opportunities for families and activities, including religious education, social justice work, and choirs.

Several challenges confront Humanism, both within and outside the UUA. Membership in mainstream Protestant denominations is declining, Evangelical growth has stalled, Catholic Church participation is falling off, while the percentage of religiously unaffiliated persons, or nones, has grown to about 20 percent. At the same time, political participation has also slid to a low of 36 percent of eligible voters in 2014. When the federal and state votes were tallied in that year, the Religious Right and its political accomplices moved well ahead, all of which runs counter to the social justice, women's rights, and religious liberty values of Unitarian Universalists.

Here are a few suggestions for confronting these challenges, in no particular order. One is that the UUA needs a more visible and active social-justice presence in Washington and on the national scene. It seems to be AWOL in the current war on public education—a battle being waged by the school pseudo-reformers, voucherizers, privatizers, profiteers, and the Religious Right—as well as the war on reproductive choice.

Another suggestion is that since at least half of us Unitarian Universalists are Humanists of one sort or another, our ministers need to show more interest in and respect for the Humanism that was largely responsible for the growth of our movement after World War II.

Finally, it would be well for Beacon Press, Skinner House Books, and *UU World* to show more interest in Humanism, especially in view of the substantial recent growth in the numbers of unaffiliated people.

Organized secular Humanism is growing. There is no good reason why UU Humanism cannot do likewise with a modicum of help from the UUA.

—◁o▷—

EDD DOERR *is president of Americans for Religious Liberty, past president of the American Humanist Association, and a widely published author on church–state separation issues.*

HUMANISM
AND RELIGIOUS
EDUCATION

Love Your Neighbor
First, Not Second

Doug Muder

A few months ago, a friend asked me to be the "guest Humanist" in the religious education class he was teaching: "Building Bridges," the course in which UU pre-teens are introduced to major world religions and philosophies.

I was told not to assume that the 11-year-olds had any prior knowledge of Humanism. What could I assume they knew? Well, my friend told me, they had already covered several other religions. He rattled off the list, and after hearing "Christianity," I decided to begin with a story about Jesus. In the Gospels, a man asks Jesus what the most important commandment is, and Jesus tells him that it's to love God. The second most important commandment, he says, is to love your neighbor.

Over the centuries, I told the kids, many different religions had come up with a similar two-step process for living a religious life.

Step one: Love God. Once that love of God is established, it motivates step two: Be good to other people.

Sometimes that works really well, particularly in communities where everyone has very similar ideas about God and how to show love for God in worship and ritual. But as the world gets more cosmopolitan, more and more often people find themselves surrounded by folks with very different ideas about God, worship, and ritual. It's far too easy for believers to get so caught up in arguments about God that they get stuck in step one, and never make it to the second step at all.

But what if, I suggested, we started at step two instead?

In a nutshell, that's the practice of Humanism: learning how to love other people, be good to them, and treat them with respect, whether they resemble us or not, and even—this part is very important—if they don't necessarily believe the same things we do.

In community, doing a proper job of loving God together requires us to agree on all sorts of contentious topics: what God is like, which books and prophets do the best job of describing God, which institutions can speak most authoritatively in God's name, and so forth.

On the other hand, feeding the hungry, healing the sick, educating the ignorant, seeking justice for the injured, and in general trying to give as many people as possible a fair shot at a satisfying life—those may not be simple jobs, but by comparison they're relatively straightforward. So let's start there.

But if we do that, what happens to the first step? Have we skipped it once and for all?

Not necessarily. When we start working together on step two, much is possible. In the cool of the evening, at the end of long days well spent, we might compare notes on the deep spiritual wells from which we draw our motivation. One person might mention Jehovah or Jesus, another Allah or Buddha, a third Reason or karma or the Form of the Good. And in the glow of the day's shared achievements, we might find ourselves listening to each other in a whole new way.

This approach allowed me to avoid the common misconceptions of Humanism, so I didn't have to lose time denying them. I'm not a diehard rationalist who ignores the softer, heart-centered parts of life. I don't resent God, or blame God for whatever's gone wrong with my life—and I don't worry about Hell.

I also avoided the big-question discussions that help other kinds of religious people categorize each other, but miss the point of Humanism. I don't know where the Universe came from, and I'm not sure what happens when people die. Even if I develop theories about such things, they'll just be my theories, not the teachings of Humanism.

So instead of talking at length about what Humanists don't believe and don't know, I managed to get right to what we're trying to do: love our neighbors. The class didn't seem to have much trouble grasping that notion.

—◄o►—

DOUG MUDER *is a contributing editor of* UU World, *and writes the political blog* The Weekly Sift *at weeklysift.com. He is a member of First Parish Unitarian Universalist in Bedford, Massachusetts.*

A Framework for
Educating Our Children

Carol Wintermute and
Kristin Wintermute

What should a Humanist-based religious education program teach our children? There are lesson plans galore in Humanist groups like Ethical Culture and some Unitarian Universalist churches and societies. Yet when considering which of these to choose from, Humanists should not start with the content of these programs. We cannot reasonably begin to cover all the topics that should be included in a Humanist religious education program in one or two hours on approximately forty Sundays a year. Even an online program has its limitations in covering all the possible topics that can be addressed.

However, in the time allotted, we can teach children about inquiry—the process of learning how to apply reason to experiences, emotions, and thoughts. This examination consists of employing critical thinking to the range of human perceptions to decipher some truths, even if impermanent, from which to begin making moral and ethical decisions. The sum of these truths and ensuing decisions form the basis of a child's emerging religious philosophy. Inquiry is the heart of the Humanist movement or life stance. Humanism is not a fixed set of ideas, principles, and so forth, to be learned and stored away. It is a process, a methodology.

Adults attend talks and discussions to have our minds and hearts stimulated. We want to hear about and discuss topics that concern us. We take in what we hear and we process it with our inventory of thoughts and experiences to create new formulations for living.

We should not deny our children access to this same process by handing them a ready-made set of thoughts and values in a fixed format. The development of their religion or life stance is our business, but the outcome is theirs. Religious literacy does not come about by reading biographies of famous Unitarians like Theodore Parker, William Ellery Channing, or Ralph Waldo Emerson. It comes from searching for a system of values and ethics that works for you in the decisions you are making now as well as in the future. We tend to look at children as potentials and fall into the trap of waiting to see if this religious education program will produce kids who graduate being able to "speak Humanism." The children are experiencing life and are making value and ethical decisions now. They are in a Humanist environment, and what they see around them is as important to their Humanist identity as is the history of Humanism.

In our Humanist communities, we do not have the time to emulate the public schools by teaching detailed, chronologically organized courses on religious history. Nor do we believe that we want to put them into the passive state of receiving information that has been prescribed as good for them to know. We can teach children the active process of evaluating the feelings, thoughts, beliefs, events, and experiences they encounter, taking into account their present stage of development, and in a nonjudgmental manner help them form their religious ideas. The goal then becomes not to teach a particular religious position, but to teach a form of religious inquiry.

To encourage this process of inquiry, we still need appropriate materials and courses. Method alone does not address the search for universal principles and purposes that underlie the diversity of the denomination. It does not address the various cognitive and affective stages of children's development.

In response to these needs, we created a comprehensive framework for developing and using present curriculum materials, which include essential subject areas and our commonly held beliefs. This framework takes into account the ages and growth stages of children and the inquiry methods that are appropriate to each developmental stage. It gives children a model for religious growth throughout their lives. Thus, the essential thrust of a Humanist religious education is to focus on expanding children's and young people's relationships.

 Five sets of relationships that help children grow can form the basis of their religious education:

Self to self: an individual's free and disciplined search for personal truth, meaning, and purpose for life. It involves developing a positive self-concept and self-worth.

Self to others: respect for the worth and dignity of other individuals and their truths, demonstrating the use of the democratic process and developing a sense of reciprocity.

Self to community: the search for insights from great prophets, thinkers, and teachers of every age and tradition in developing social contracts with neighbors, school-mates, children of other religions, and members of one's community.

Self to the natural environment: respect for all of life and a sense of responsibility for the earth and its resources now and in the future.

Self to the future: the development of oneself as a citi-zen of the world, striving for a world community of love, reason, justice, and peace.

Also underlying the framework are developmental levels that assume human beings go through various stages of thinking and feeling in their lifetime. Each stage incorpo-rates the former stage, thereby increasing the complexity of responses individuals have at their disposal in reaction to their thoughts, experiences, emotions, and beliefs. The stages are incremental, not hierarchical. The pre-adult levels of development in this framework are steps between differentiating one's ideas and experiences and integrating them with one's worldview.

- Level I, 3 to 4 years old: The undifferentiated belief of the infant (from birth to 2 years old) moves to trust bonding with family and significant others.
- Level II, 5 to 7 years old: A child's belief imitates the family's beliefs, outlook, and ethical behavior.
- Levels IIIa and IIIb, 7 to 9, and 9 to 11 years old, respectively: A child's concrete belief is based on myth, legend, and stories of prophetic visionaries as part of one's community heritage and tradition.
- Levels IVa and IVb, 11 to 14, and 14 to 18 years old, respectively: A tested belief is developed as a result of encountering, belonging to, and sharing with the peer group in one's community. This includes sharing the group's symbols, stories, meanings, and traditions.

An infinite number of topics within these five incremental relationships and developmental levels can be selected for the focus of inquiry. The sciences, technology, arts, and humanities are appropriate disciplines to use for this purpose.

The humanities include history, literature, and philosophy and these are based on the study of texts and ideas rather than on observing the external world or on experimentation. Science and technology, on the other hand, are based on observation and quantification. Together, all these studies instill a critical attitude toward all knowledge claims and prepare students to sort through the mass of complex issues facing them in the near future.

Appropriate subject areas for a Humanist religious education include:

- The Humanist life stance: examining human nature, the history and philosophy of Humanism, and the various kinds of Humanism.
- Humanist values and principles: understanding moral and ethical positions.
- Humanism in relation to world religions: becoming acquainted with the principles of other religions.
- Critical thinking: determining knowledge and truth.
- Physical and life sciences: understanding scientific methods and uses and the body of knowledge uncovered by science.
- Social science: identifying social, political, and legal issues.
- Contemporary culture: looking at the "isms" that affect our culture and our relationship with others and issues of current concern.
- Leadership: determining what constitutes being a leader, and practicing how to be effective in following your personal and institutional ethics and mission.
- Aesthetics: expressing Humanism through the arts, and creating Humanist events and celebrations.

When you combine the five forms of relationship, the developmental levels of children and young adults, and the domains of knowledge, you have a framework for lesson plans and courses for a Humanistic religious education program. Many subjects can be dealt with on several levels, with increased complexity as children grow.

The framework on the following pages consists of forty-five modules.

In his article "Humanist Education," Nimrod Aloni from Hakibbutzim College of Education, Israel, writes that the aim of Humanist religious educators is to help children become well-rounded and integrated people "so that the 'tree of knowledge' would also serve as a nourishing 'tree of life.'" Besides helping children balance their cultural integration and their individuality, Humanistic teachers should "set [a] personal example in the art of living" and ensure an atmosphere of "care, trust, dialogue, respect, fairness, tolerance, inquiry, freedom, commitment, responsibility, multiculturalism and reciprocity. Without these last elements, even the most beautifully woven theory of humanistic education would fail to become a live reality for its teacher and students."

Religious education from a Humanist perspective is all about learning the process of inquiry. It involves applying reason to feelings, thoughts, and experiences to find meaning and then determining the appropriate content for helping children and young people make moral and ethical decisions that affirm themselves, others, and our planet.

Curriculum Modules for Religious Education

Developmental level (age)	Relationships				
	Self	Others	Community	Environment	World
VII (Adult)	Committing to a continuous religious inquiry	Acting as an ethical being in relationships	Exemplifying one's religious principles by leadership	Assuming leadership in developing a system of ethics	Evoking a sense of universal compassion: love, reason, justice, and peace
VI (Adult)	Accepting the value of one's religious tradition	Accepting the value of others' moral and ethical positions	Affirming one's religious position	Accepting responsibility for the environment	Defining one's role in service to humankind
V (18–Adult)	Reflecting on one's own religious odyssey	Reflecting on one's ethical behavior toward others	Reflecting on principles and purposes in religion	Reflecting on one's attitudes and actions toward the natural world	Reflecting on one's involvement in the cause of humankind

	Daring to be oneself	Acknowledging responsibility for one's actions	Daring to represent one's religious view in a group	Accepting responsibility for the earth and its resources	Exploring attitudes toward humankind
IVb (14–18)	Daring to be oneself	Acknowledging responsibility for one's actions	Daring to represent one's religious view in a group	Accepting responsibility for the earth and its resources	Exploring attitudes toward humankind
IVa (11–14)	Developing the freedom to express oneself	Developing a system of ethics toward others	Seeking shared values in other religions	Distinguishing various environmental policies	Distinguishing religious world visions
IIIb (9–11)	Identifying with real-life experience	Identifying with people's attitudes toward others	Identifying with people who advocate equality	Exploring lives that exemplify responsibility to the earth	Exploring lives that have created a worldview
IIIa (7–9)	Recognizing oneself in stories or myths	Recognizing others' rights and worth through stories or myths	Discovering the democratic process in history and legend	Exploring stories and theories of science and nature	Exploring stories striving for world community
II (5–7)	Identifying oneself and one's family with church	Identifying ethical behavior toward others	Identifying different religious ideas	Identifying the need to care for nature	Identifying cultures that are part of one's heritage
I (3–4)	Discovering oneself	Discovering others	Discovering the church	Discovering nature	Discovering the world's children

—◦—

The late **CAROL WINTERMUTE** *was co-dean of the Humanist Institute and was director of religious education of the First Unitarian Society of Minneapolis for many years.*

KRISTIN WINTERMUTE *is executive director of the Humanist Institute.*

THE IMPORTANCE
OF COMMUNITY

Humanism Is Community

Emerson Zora Hamsa

A Black Christian church seems an odd place for Humanism to find its roots, but my Humanism is firmly rooted in the African Methodist Episcopal Zion Church. Yes, my Humanism flourished in the midst of Bible-quoting, Bible-believing Christians who cared deeply about each other and about life itself and who worked together to make meaning in a world in which they had been othered, marginalized, and all but rendered invisible by the pervasiveness of antiblack white supremacy. Perhaps, without even knowing it, these beautiful people of faith planted the seeds of my Humanism. They modeled for me the possibilities for practicing the kind of Humanism that relies upon human activity to make change in the world and seeks pleasure and joy in the struggle against injustice. They taught me that Humanism is the work that we do—and the practices we cultivate—that help us survive and thrive in the midst of the absurdity of existence. The church family of my childhood is the reason that the Humanism that guides my life is rooted in the love and care of other human beings. My Humanist approach to living prioritizes practices of community. The love and care that were given to me and required of me during my childhood in the A.M.E. Zion Church epitomizes the roots of my Humanist practices today.

As I think back on those days, a particular memory comes to mind: When I was just shy of twelve years old, the deacons at Saint Mark African Methodist Episcopal Zion Church elected me as the church's youngest junior delegate to attend our denomination's most prestigious conference: The General Conference of African Methodist Episcopal Zion Churches. That year, the conference was held in Birmingham, Alabama, a Southern city worlds away from my home in upstate New York. What I remember most about this opportunity isn't the conference itself, but the practices of community that led to me attending it. Sister May (not her real name), the church Sunday School superintendent, invested considerable time and resources into making sure I was protected and cared for during my time away from home. In many ways, my bearing witness to Sister May's care and kindness planted the seeds for what would ultimately blossom into my own understanding of the ways in which Humanism relies upon the constant activity of human beings. In other words, Sister May taught me to recognize what is possible when human beings are responsible and accountable to each other.

After the deacon board's decision to send me to Birmingham, Sister May went about the business of finding a suitable chaperone for me. She insisted that I stay by her side as she made phone calls to people throughout the district, in search of a responsible adult who would be able to fly a thousand miles with me from New York to Alabama. Almost daily, she talked with other Christian women whom she felt were capable of "keeping an eye on me" at the conference. She sought someone who would make sure I was well-behaved, well-fed, and back in my hotel room as soon as evening worship ended each night. Someone, she said, who would treat me "like her own child."

Sister May did not know she was teaching me how to live and practice Humanism. "You need to know how to do the Lord's work," she said to me, as she folded plain sheets of notebook paper down the middle and wrote a potential chaperone's name and phone number on each sheet. At the top of each column, she alternately wrote the words *pros* and *cons*. I watched her talk enthusiastically on the phone with each woman, stopping the conversation to scribble notes on either side of the paper as she listened to their responses. After each call, she turned to me, handed me the sheet of paper, and announced her verdict: "Sister Diana ain't even going to conference this year. She would have been a good somebody to send you with." Or, "Sister Anna does not sound sure of her yes. And you know what the Word of the Lord says about the double-minded man."

Sister May finally received a call from Sister Glover, a public high school principal from a nearby town. Sister Glover was planning to take a youth group to the General Conference. She agreed to allow me to travel with her group under the condition that Sister May and I attend the junior delegate training sessions at her home during the months leading up to the conference. Sister May agreed, and later that month we began our ritual weekend drives to junior delegate training.

When Sister May made those calls to woman after woman after woman until she found someone who would care for me in Alabama, she was—I now understand— modeling Humanist principles. She showed me that the only way to truly see God move—however we conceive of God—is through the activity of human beings. All those years ago, Sister May showed me that simply praying for my safety, without actively searching for someone to care for me, would have been an empty gesture. She modeled for me that love, care, and protection were available only through the active participation of the community around me.

When I reflect upon this experience, and I often do, I realize that Sister May and Sister Glover's actions actually taught me to let go of God. They taught me that what *we do* matters, and that it is what we do that influences the world around us. These two Christian women taught me that it is the responsibility of human beings to care for each other and to struggle in community against living mean-ingless lives. Unbeknownst to them, Sister May and Sister

Glover taught me that people are indeed capable of working out their own salvation. In other words, our practices of community sustain us and give meaning to our lives. They taught me that human beings are fully and ultimately accountable for how we practice our humanity in the world. As a younger person, I struggled with whether I *could be* a Humanist. I thought that *being Humanist* meant that I had to eschew all things theist and take up the cause of "proving" that there is no God. It seemed to me that being Humanist meant turning away from the very community that taught me how to live according to Humanist commitments. But living a Humanist life has not meant any of those things to me. In fact, living a Humanist life has meant embracing the ways in which we all—as part of the interdependent web of existence—are responsible for making meaning, finding joy, and actively working toward individual and social transformation in a world that I believe contains no inherent meaning.

Humanism is the way I honor the radical love, work, and yes, even the faith of my ancestors. I did not know that the process of watching elder Black women work to send me to a conference would change everything I ever thought about God and religion. But it did. And I could not have imagined that experience would inform the Humanist principles that guide my life. But it did that too. And now Humanism is one of the primary ways that influences how I grapple with hard questions about the ways our bodies, race, gender, sexuality, justice, and thoughts about (yes)

God help us face the sometimes overwhelming existential questions of our collective existence—who, what, where, and why are we here?

To some, my claim that the roots of my Humanism were firmly established in the A.M.E. Zion Church may seem antithetical to the Humanist enterprise itself. However, the Humanist approach to living that I have chosen allows me to maintain a deep appreciation for the cultural significance of Black theistic religions. Because of this, I can respect the ways that faith-centered communities grapple with the same existential questions that Humanists do when Humanists search for meaning while simultaneously working toward a world in which democracy—without respect for any particular religion—can flourish. My hope for Unitarian Universalism is that we fully embrace a Humanism that is expansive enough to never absolve itself of the responsibility to love and care for all people. This is the call of—and to—Humanism. My hope is that we heed this call again and again—not by simply quoting our seven Principles during our worship celebrations, but by practicing the kind of Humanism in which our activity in the world always reminds us that we cannot survive this life without each other.

‹o›

EMERSON ZORA HAMSA *is a candidate for ministerial fellowship in the Unitarian Universalist Association and a doctoral student in the Department of Religion at Rice University in Houston, Texas.*

A Path Toward Wholeness

Kaaren Anderson

I fell in love with Humanism in high school at the Unitarian Meeting House in Madison, Wisconsin. The minister, Max Gaebler, shared his intellectual Humanism with a caring, enlivened sense of being in the world. He was a witty, charming man, who at five feet six in dress shoes seemed to have emerged from the illustrated pages of Clement Clarke Moore's classic, as Gaebler was a real, live, jolly old elf. Gaebler and the Unitarian Meeting House proved a balm for my sin-sick soul.

Previously, I had sung in a Congregational church choir directed by my father alongside quirky elders with rascally rabbit pitch they couldn't quite trap. In that congregation, I often felt the beguiling love and warmth of community, but more often than not, I couldn't reconcile the various leaps of faith with anything rational or true.

I confess to unabashedly copying my friend Martha's answers from her confirmation class homework sheet onto my own in the backseat of her parents' Buick on the way to church. My goal was to be confirmed solely to attain a prized family heirloom from my Lutheran grandmother. With the class complete and my having been anointed—confirmed—the ring was mine, and like Gollum in *The Lord of the Rings*, I had made a deal with my own devil of deceit, greed, and shallowness for a worldly good rather than a spiritual one.

The Meeting House, on the other hand, did not ask me for leaps of faith. Rather, it asked me to align my actions in accord with age-old truths of loving my neighbor as myself and serving needs greater than my own. It didn't ask me to believe in a god who was seemingly capricious and arbitrary. It didn't ask me to not ask questions; instead it told me that curiosity is the blessed gift of the holy and that, somewhere within and beside others, answers can and do arise. I was indeed home. From ninth grade on, I have proudly worn the badge of Humanism as an emblem of the good life. It made intellectual sense to me. Then, when I was thirty-two, something happened and everything changed.

I was serving my first parish in Rockport, Massachusetts. I was in a brand-new, long-distance relationship. For a number of reasons, I was stressed and felt overwhelmed most of that summer and fall. I developed one strep infection after another, took many rounds of antibiotics, yet the bouts of sickness kept on coming.

By January, I had come down with a strep pneumonia infection (the same thing that had killed the puppeteer Jim Henson). It was filling up all the pockets in my neck with infection and constraining my wind pipe. I barely survived emergency surgery, and my family was called to be with me in what had the potential to be the last hours of my life. Each day, my love, my sister, and my brother-in-law were at my side, calming me down, explaining various procedures and my medical care, holding my hand, kissing my forehead.

The third night in the ICU, I panicked. It felt like my throat was closing up again. I had this unshakable feeling that I was going to die, right then and there. As I wrestled for some sense of self control, I remember staring up at the ceiling, with the air vents pumping and an EKG clicking, and I thought, "This is it. This is the end."

And then it happened. This calm, this blanket of comfort, enveloped me, and I said out loud in my head, "You know what, if I die now, it's okay. It is. I've lived a good life, and all that matters is, I'm loved and I love. How lucky am I. I'm loved." I did not call out to a god to save me or to a magical force to remind me that there is something after this reality as we know it—some life to be reborn into. Being loved was sufficient; it was . . . enough.

So here's the thing: This was the moment of my reckoning regarding belief. But it was more as well. It was the marking of when I really became a Humanist. Up until that time, my belief in humans as the agency for one's salvation and transformation was theory. It was reason, conjecture, perhaps even a little leap of faith. But there, in the ICU, my Humanism moved from an intellectual construct to a force that solidified itself deep within me. It became more than a theory or an intellectual construct; it became part of me. It is me. Both intellect and heart, woven into my understanding of the world.

For a long time now, I haven't believed in a god with a will, intentionality, or consciousness. I don't put all my eggs in the basket of a god who will save and transform me. Rather, I look to humans, to my relationships with people.

Transcendence with life, with the holy, comes through my human relationships. And yes, I get that humans will let me down and will hurt me as well. They will disappoint, betray, and otherwise fail me. But they also have repeatedly saved me from a selfish me-ism that can destroy my well-being and lead me to false idols. They have loved me so fiercely that I am brought back from despair, loneliness, and isolation. They have cajoled me into my better self, when, frankly, I sometimes don't want to bother with the effort. They have challenged me to aspire to possibilities that I fear are unobtainable, because they see something in me that I far too often can't see in myself. They are human. They are the four Fs: flawed, fragile, f*#&!d up, and, most importantly, fabulous. This understanding is the Humanism that has transcended the intellect, buried itself inside me, and inspires and heals me daily.

My Humanism/nontheism is rooted in right behavior, not creeds. Science tells us that, surprisingly, our behavior influences our reason, not the other way around. So if our intellectualism doesn't influence our living and loving, our good—with or without god—what use is it?

The mission of the church I recently served, The First Unitarian Church of Rochester, is to create spiritual connection by listening to our deepest voice, opening to life's gifts, and serving needs greater than our own.

Our church is rooted in the belief that evil is disconnection—disconnection from self, others, and the oneness of life. For us, it's not about belief. It doesn't matter if you are a theist, an atheist, an agnostic, a Pagan, a Buddhist, a Christian, or a Barnes-and-Noble-ite. If your beliefs are in service to connection, then they are in. If they aren't, then they are out. It's that simple.

In some ways, this way of understanding the world is ancient. In her provocative book *The Great Transformation*, Karen Armstrong points to the Axial Age, when this concept was made manifest. She explains that for the sages of the time, what mattered "was not what you believed but how you behaved. Religion was about doing things that changed you at a profound level. The only way you could encounter what they called 'God' was to live a compassionate life. Indeed, religion was compassion."

This precept is a guiding force for my Humanism. It reminds me that the religious life has more to do with being humble, and with being deeply connected to oneself, others, and the needs of the world, than it does anything else. It means that empathy, kindness, justice-making, forgiveness, reconciliation, and restraining from judgment are essential to being and experiencing a vitality of the life force that runs through each of us.

My Humanism/nontheism is rooted in the idea that as Humanists, as Unitarian Universalists, we are a part of a living tradition—one that cares about living well in this life rather than paying attention to the possible next. But this focus on today's life doesn't mean that what comes after this life doesn't freak the bejesus out of most people.

After twenty years in the ministry, I've seen enough fear in people's eyes when they are close to death; I know that death can terrify folks. It is hard to fathom the end of one's consciousness. So we often say it is up to each of us to decide for ourselves what comes next. We are concerned with this life, not the next. Yet, often that isn't a very satisfying answer.

But here's the thing: I think we have an answer. The answer for what is comforting and what supports us at death is science. It is thermodynamics, it is physics, it is biology, it is evolution. We are always still connected, as we have always been. I just got a tattoo on my arm to remind me that I've got today—now—to live. But it also reminds me that I am connected. It says, "From stardust I arrived, to dust I shall return."

From stardust I arrived, to dust I shall return. Science keeps me grounded and somewhat less afraid of death. And on some level, there is something almost ethereal and mind-blowing that we are all connected—that the molecules we breathe in include argon, which we shared with the Buddha and Jesus and that mischievous Eve in the garden. Science is our answer to soften the blow of annihilation and the abyss.

My Humanism/nontheism is rooted in the metaphor of the cracked pot. What is the fear about being broken? We are all broken. Not in an inherently sinful way, but in the way that any life worth living and fighting for comes with a fair amount of knocks—both unearned and sometimes earned. So, we are broken somehow; we are not perfect. I say bless that uniquely, infinitely human condition, because ultimately it is our imperfections that bond us to one another, not the other way around.

Truth is, accepting this communal brokenness isn't as scary as we think, especially when we can do it together. We should talk about brokenness because we are in pain about it. We think we should be all things to all people or think that we can't fail. We try to keep a stiff upper lip and not let anyone see how fragile we feel, because if we did, we might not know how to keep going on. We might have lost our job, partner, child, marriage, well-being, hope, or compass for what is good and right. We might have compromised our values to fit in. We are insecure, lonely, hurting, and lost.

Yes, we are broken, but my Humanism says, so what? I am often broken, yet pieced together. Sometimes the duct tape and glue of our healing process holds us together. Sometimes another's love has transformed my hurt so thoroughly that there remains only the remnants of a once-raw scar. The point is, when we can just sink into this, we can be less lonely, less afraid, less disconnected. Together, in the company and love of one another, we can be made whole.

This is my Humanism. Not singularly intellectual. Not steeped in certitude. But a relentlessly relational, ruthlessly real, test-driven-by-near-death Humanism. Humanism of holy stardust and ash. Of brokenness and wholeness.

◄o►

KAAREN ANDERSON *has served four Unitarian Universalist congregations as minister, most recently The First Unitarian Church of Rochester, New York. She currently is artist/owner/ designer of Solveig Studio.*

SHARING STORIES

T. K. BARGER

When I describe Unitarian Universalism, I use the metaphor of the spiritual journey. I say that the Unitarian Universalist approach is that all people are on spiritual journeys. We don't all have the same route or even the same destination, but it's a joy to travel together when our paths meet, to support one another in our spiritual seeking—and sometimes finding—and to share stories along the way.

Those stories are Humanism in practice, people to people. The stories include scripture, literary tales, and even Internet memes. We're sharing our stories with others, recognizing the wonder of being human. That is religious Humanism.

Many religious Humanists join Unitarian Universalist congregations to be with other Humanists honoring that awe. We walk together recognizing that it's up to us humans to make the world a better place, to support one another in the joys and concerns of living a full and loving life, and even to interpret a spiritual dimension of Humanism.

The word spiritual, like the quality it is meant to describe, can be hazy. It isn't solidly determined in a scientific manner. In this way, it's like the human condition; we are many kinds of good and bad, subjectively so, according to many philosophies, morals, and theologies, and tempered by so many belief systems other than Humanism. Spiritual is related to faith tradition—a set of customs or beliefs subscribed to by a large group of people, be it Buddhism, an Abrahamic religion, a particular denominationalism, or atheism and other no-faith paths.

Unlike some Humanists I don't consider myself "spiritual but not religious." Awe, to me, is a religious feeling, and being with other Humanists rather than going it alone with books and online exploration makes practicing my Humanism a religious exercise.

Some Humanists may say they're spiritual but not religious partly because they see the damage that people, governments, and organizations have done in the name of religion throughout recorded history. Others reject spirit and religion. I describe Humanism as both spiritual and religious, but I understand that this language doesn't fit for all of us.

Humanism continues to have vocabulary challenges. The term has been applied differently through the ages, to concepts that sometimes link up with today's religious and secular Humanisms. The usage isn't consistent today, either. Some people proclaim a Humanism that includes everybody as potential Humanists—the common denominator is being human. Others insist it means a kind of atheism that excludes nonbelievers who might be open to discussing entities or ideas that include the term god.

Another approach says that Humanism is religious without relying on or otherwise recognizing anything supernatural. It maintains that what we know is based on science and direct experience, and that the unknown may eventually be discovered and explained. Science is important to Humanists, especially the scientific method, but Humanism isn't scientism.

What all Humanists have in common with more traditional religious adherents is not a god, but a love for stories—ancient, contemporary, common, and individual. Some stories, even Humanists' awe-filled stories, are solidly spiritual.

My use of the term spiritual might annoy some Humanists who want to strip away traditional religious language. What I mean is with thoughts, emotions, or feelings or in some other way, all humans look beyond themselves or examine inwardly, and stand in awe at being part of existence. We can be together as people experiencing our different kinds of awe, talking about it while living in the world, with honor and dignity toward self and others, in a way that makes life worthwhile and the planet thriving for future generations.

That which we have in common does not have to be God; we all can have awe in common. For Humanists, Unitarian Universalism provides a place where we can be together while still sharing our differences.

I learned about Humanism and its philosophical history as a student at Hendrix College in Conway, Arkansas, in the late 1970s. I wrote a paper about David Hume, a forebear of today's secular and religious Humanism.

I first heard about secular Humanism on talk radio in Austin, Texas. It was about 1981, and political conversation was taking over AM stations. Evangelicals had been an instrumental bloc in Ronald Reagan's election as president, and on the air, talk-show hosts and their callers were developing fundamentalist us-versus-them distinctions. On that frequency, born-again Christians were good, and secular Humanists were bad.

The radio callers and hosts spoke about the Humanist Manifesto. I was attracted to the conversation as one of "them," not the talk show's "us." I wanted to learn more about the Humanist perspective and renew the philosophical ties from my college studies. I knew my interests in Humanism wouldn't be aired on those conservative radio programs.

Almost a decade later, I started attending a Unitarian Universalist church and became a member in 1992. There I learned about the distinction between secular Humanism and religious Humanism, and realized that I'm a religious Humanist.

Once I discovered that Humanist-oriented ministry could be a professional calling, I entered both the Humanist Institute and Meadville Lombard Theological School in 2006. In my studies, I was inspired by some of the Unitarian minister pioneers of twentieth-century Humanism, including Curtis Reese, John Dietrich, and Edwin Wilson, who was one of the founders of the American Humanist Association. With my background in publishing, I naturally saw my own potential in light of the lives and writings of these men.

Reese was among a group of Americans who in the early 1900s applied Humanism specifically to religion, developing a Humanist theology that became dominant in the Unitarian movement in the mid-twentieth century. He was a theologian and an administrator working with ministers —some of whom held his beliefs, and others who didn't. When his nontheistic Humanist theology was attacked, he was defended by theist ministers who appreciated his work, and Unitarianism affirmed its creedlessness as a result.

As dean of the Abraham Lincoln Centre in Chicago, Reese wrote extensively for its publication, *Unity*, and published four books on Humanism between 1926 and 1945. He also headed the editorial team that developed the Humanist Manifesto of 1933. I take from Reese an appreciation of others' approaches to Humanism that don't completely match mine. I also remain open to the religious pluralism of fellow Unitarian Universalists and the possibility of exploring our individual theologies together.

John Dietrich, often credited as the founder of religious Humanism, was the longtime minister of First Unitarian Society of Minneapolis, where I served a ministerial internship in 2008 and 2009. During my time in the Twin Cities, I studied Dietrich's Humanism using the society's archives and resources at the Minnesota Historical Society.

Edwin Wilson, managing editor of *The New Humanist*, which published the Humanist Manifesto of 1933, was also one of its signers. His work in establishing the American Humanist Association institutionalized Humanism, and his publishing of Humanist magazines gave the movement a forum. He was one of the authors of the 1973 Humanist Manifesto II, revisiting Humanism in light of the changes wrought over the four intervening decades.

As is true for many movements, Humanism was largely developed by white men. As a Humanist, I can recognize the origins and foundation of my three Unitarian Humanist forebears and others, and seek inspiration across gender, race, and culture. I look for diversity in sex, race, and situation from their time until now, and promote wider acceptance of all others in the future.

My mentor in the Humanist Institute class was Kendyl Gibbons, who during my final year at Meadville Lombard supervised my ministerial internship in Minneapolis, where she served as senior minister at the time. As a student, I was the managing editor of the *Journal of Liberal Religion* at Meadville Lombard for three years, working with Bill Murry, then president of the school, and published in the journal an article on Meadville Lombard's connections to the Humanist Manifesto.

Like the pioneers in a religious Humanism movement that entered the public consciousness in the late nineteenth century and came into its own in the twentieth, I have Humanism at the core of my religious identification.

As a Unitarian Universalist minister who has a Humanist orientation, I relate with people, regardless of religion, philosophy, or orientation. I can rely on our common humanity to walk with them in times of joy or grief. In sermons I can illustrate similarities and differences in issues, dilemmas, ways of being religious, and so much more. And I can respect the people who are neither Humanists nor Unitarian Universalists who have firm foundations in their religions' key figures. This is because we have religion in common and stories to share.

I also have been a journalist who covered religion. For more than four years I was the religion editor for *The Blade*, the daily newspaper in Toledo, Ohio. A reporter who is a Humanist has a good perspective from which to approach the multifaith world. I start with what we have in common, our being people in this world. By appreciating stories, I try to give dignity and honor to the people and religious organizations I profile and to the sources in the news articles I write. If they talk about God, I do not establish our differences. I try to reach their humanness. For my opinion columns, I write from my Humanist perspective and try to be open and have common ground with many readers.

It doesn't violate me personally to write about a person's belief in supernatural phenomena that I don't subscribe to. My journalism is not a conversion game; I'm not interested in convincing the other that I'm right or opening myself to their theological way. It's a conversation in which I hope we learn more about people, the way we are, and how we improve parts of our world, and what we might come to believe.

My religious journalism is grounded in stories, with the awareness that the potential readers are from many faith traditions and communities. It's also based on my own curiosity about this world, its people, their ideas, and their sacred ways. And I'm always aware that the breadth of religion includes no religion. As a journalist, as a minister, and as an individual, I base my spiritual journey on my Humanism.

My UU Humanist orientation as a religious person helps me observe and be open to the ways of others. I'm comfortable in my faith when comfort is important. I'm uncomfortable in it as both a seeker and as a person who knows that so much more must be done to change the world.

And I get to seek out, hear, and tell stories. What we do with our stories is a main concern of Humanism. Humanists are mindful that we're responsible for change, that this world is the one we know. We're responsible for the stories that aren't based on experience, knowing that it's people who make up the characters, the settings, and the narratives. These stories can entertain and educate.

It's all on us. I urge all of us on our spiritual journeys to share stories. That's where religion and Humanism meet.

◄◊►

T.K. BARGER *is the interim minister at First Unitarian Church of Toledo, in Ohio. Previously, he worked as a writer and editor in Austin, Texas; New York City; and Toledo, where he was a reporter, feature writer, and columnist for* The Blade.

Religious but Not Spiritual

Kevin Jagoe

A millennial is someone who was born between 1982 and 2004 and who grew up in the computer age. People often see this group as simultaneously entrepreneurial, self-centered, work-avoidant, and able to solve the world's problems—possibly from our parents' basements. As one of those millennials, who everyone from the media to parents to congregations loves to covet as well as bemoan, I'm trying to be uniquely conventional by living my life as best as I can.

I am a very unlikely churchgoer. For most of my life, I've thought that there wasn't room for me within religious spaces or religious traditions. I'm young and gay, I have no children, and I'm an atheist. The belief that church wasn't for me stayed with me until early adulthood, when I unexpectedly applied to work for a church. The decision was a major fork in my life's path, one that I am just beginning to understand.

I graduated from Hamline University, a small liberal-arts school in Saint Paul, Minnesota. While a student there, I began to explore my beliefs and move beyond the negative experiences I'd had as a child and teen within a conservative church. That environment, which discouraged questioning and advocated instead a recitation of doctrine, held little room for my nascent gay and atheist identities. Only from outside the religious community of my childhood did I begin to see that to become the person I needed to be, I would need a better community to stand within.

Throughout my college years, I worked to create a better community on campus for lesbian, gay, bisexual, and transgender students as well as for non-majority religious communities. I helped usher in two new housing programs: one within the dorms through gender-neutral housing and one outside the dorms through a house for LGBT students. I also helped start the first student group at Hamline to focus on religious identities with an Earth Spiritual or Pagan worldview. I was invited by the group's founders to help lead them through the challenges of creating a funded student group and was happy to be seen as a religious ally for the students working on building community for others.

With graduation from college came the search for a second part-time job. So I applied for an open position at First Universalist Church of Minneapolis. I had spent much of the time since leaving home focused on building communities for others and myself. I hadn't spent much time at all reflecting on the wounds my earlier encounters with churches had left. This church job was perfect. It was well located, paid relatively well, and used all the skills I had been developing in communications work for nonprofits. However, it was a church. I decided to do more research about it before applying. I had no idea what a Universalist church could be. I ultimately spent more than an hour clicking from entry to entry and website to website about this particular congregation as well as the larger tradition it represented. What I found led me to apply for the position. I wasn't convinced I would fit, but I would at least have a better experience than I had in previous places called churches.

This congregation exemplified a positive religious community. I could see the good this place did for both its members and the larger world around it. I also began to think again about my atheist identity and the need for something more. A minister suggested that I visit another Unitarian Universalist congregation two miles away from where I worked. I attended a few Sunday services and discovered a whole building full of self-identified Humanists. This group of people reflected the thoughts I had been carrying with me for more than a decade and shared my beliefs—or lack thereof—about the divine. It also shared my beliefs about our world. Through my experiences at First Unitarian Society of Minneapolis, I began to discover how being an atheist, a Humanist, a gay man, and a Unitarian Universalist were all possible simultaneously. All the pieces of me could fit within those walls, and I could bring my full self to volunteering within a religious context. From this place of healing, I also began to see myself fitting within the larger fabric of Unitarian Universalism. The Humanist influences were evident within the community I was employed by, and many traditions came together in both these UU communities.

My personal theology or worldview has three parts: My answer to the question about God, gods, or a higher power is atheism. My answer to how I should live my life is Humanism. My answer to where I can practice my beliefs, find community, and grow into a better person with others is Unitarian Universalism. I also believe that life is a vocation —not just my life, but everyone's. All human beings have a calling to do something of worth in this world, and this world is the only chance people have to discover and live out that calling. We have a short amount of time to find joy, create community, do something to help our fellow humans, and leave behind something to be remembered.

The sense of learning from the different perspectives and paths of others is why I find my Humanist home in the Unitarian Universalist tradition. I enjoy discovering the many ways people find truth and meaning in their lives. I am inspired not only to learn from their point of view but also to think critically about my own beliefs and reevaluate whether they are the best way to interpret what I see in the world. My theology is neither fixed nor solid. As I grow and experience life, I may still be a Humanist, but the exact way I define my Humanism and view those around me may change. Having a community that in its principles accepts this spectrum of belief is important.

After participating both as a congregant and a staff person within Unitarian Universalist congregations, I wanted to learn more about my philosophical history as a Humanist. I needed to find a way to deepen my roots, and the occasional adult religious education program or self-guided reading list did not seem sufficient. The Humanist Institute, a three-year graduate program, offered a structured way to explore Humanism broadly and in depth. There I could freely explore the history of Humanism and the present-day Humanist movement. I also came to better appreciate the religious community I belonged to as I heard the stories of teachers and other students at the institute. During this time, I began to entertain the idea of ministry as my own vocation and a viable career path. Many religious leaders have held Humanist ideas and led institutions or served communities in a variety of ways. In their stories, I could see pieces of myself. As I heard more stories and met people from around the world doing similar work, I gradually leaned toward this work of creating meaningful community for people who might not fit into traditional molds.

My deepest religious questions have little to do with the nature of the divine or with humanity's relationship to any deities that may shape our world. My questions have everything to do with our relationships with each other. How do we tell our stories and remember the lessons of our collective heritage? How do we live out our lives and leave legacies we can be proud of for future generations? How do we as individuals make decisions that make, and build on, positive change in the world around us? These questions, not very different from those of others who are seeking to lead communities, help hold the stories of our past within a religious context. The deepest lessons in religion help us better relate to our neighbors in the here and now. If I believe in any supernatural force in the universe that cannot be measured or fully understood by science, it is human potential. Human beings continue to do amazing and powerful things. Some of these things are destructive, but the more powerful actions create, reimagine, and change our world into something better.

Writer, director, and producer Joss Whedon described his faith in humanity when he accepted the Outstanding Lifetime Achievement Award in Cultural Humanism from the Humanist Community at Harvard. He said, "Faith in humanity means believing absolutely in something with a huge amount of proof to the contrary. We are the true believers." I believe deeply in the potential of human beings, and Humanism gives a voice to those who see the great depth and value of people, not as divinely significant or cosmically special, but precious simply for being human and being here.

Now as a seminarian studying at Meadville Lombard School of Theology, I strive to continue to learn more about my religious forebears. I may have found them as an adult, but I feel as though I were dropped into the religious tradition of my birth by accident, only to realize as an adult where I truly belong. There is a long history to our tradition, and I hope to share it with others. Much of my professional work has involved sharing the stories of other communities and helping to create spaces for people to more fully become who they hope to be. For a long time, I saw no place where I could do this work and bring to it everything I am. Ministry is a vocation that does all of this and more.

Much of the work I want to do, I could easily do in a secular community center or with a variety of nonprofit organizations that prioritize safety and inclusiveness. But there is something else happening in religious spaces that secular spaces lack: the passing on of an ethical heritage, a temporal tradition, and a place to develop into a morally mature individual. It is through communities like congregations that these things happen. These spaces are set aside for people to learn about the past, develop practices to be more grounded in the present, and, through their participation, pass something on to those who will come in the future. Communities like First Universalist Church and First Unitarian Society have made a mark on the world around them. They have helped countless people who have never set foot in their buildings or who don't know what Unitarian Universalism means. These communities share a heritage that welcomes the stranger, the thinker, the activist, and the whole person.

Not all my questions about identity and belief have yet been completely answered. And once I think I've come close to an answer, entirely new questions arise. The journey of a questioning mind does not have a destination; it has many stops along the way. I am grateful that the path of UU Humanism will guide me along this journey of discovery.

—◦—

KEVIN JAGOE *is youth director at the First Unitarian Society of Minneapolis and a ministerial student at Meadville Lombard Theological School.*

BEYOND
UNITARIAN UNIVERSALISM

CHRIS STEDMAN

While a number of atheists and Humanists excitedly champion the news that more and more Americans are identifying as nonreligious, I'm concerned. As a Humanist, I worry that the growing number of nonreligious young people won't have communities to turn to in times of crisis and need, or spaces to interact with and learn from people who can inspire and challenge them to engage with questions of meaning and purpose. This concern is a big part of why, after a nonreligious childhood and a deeply religious adolescence, I now work to build community for nonreligious people. Although I certainly can't speak for the needs and interests of every nonreligious millennial, much of what I've learned comes from conversations I've had while working with students at Yale, Harvard, and the U.S. colleges and universities I've visited as a speaker over the last six years.

I grew up not just nonreligious, but irreligious. I was baptized in a Methodist church, but the event was really just an excuse to get the family together to celebrate a new arrival. Its theological significance was essentially nonexistent, and it was always described in secular terms in the years that followed. As a kid, I didn't hear the word God in my house—but I didn't hear the word atheist, either. My family just wasn't religious, and the topic didn't come up much.

My family flirted with Unitarian Universalism while I was in the fourth grade, and we began attending a family friend's church. The church was vibrant and offered its congregants much by way of moral reflection and communal support, and I enjoyed playing games and making friends in Sunday school. The church was thirty minutes away, though, and my family and I had a lot on our plates; before long, we stopped making the trip.

In fifth grade, I read Alex Haley's *Roots*, a novel tracing one family's history through American slavery. I was mortified that something so horrific and so inhumane could happen, let alone in my own country's recent history. I remember vividly how I sat on my bed and sobbed—that such injustice could exist in the world at all and that the wrong would go so largely unchallenged ripped open a hole in my gut that exists to this day.

I had no framework for responding to this disequilibrium, no language to begin articulating some of the questions that formulated as I continued to read. Slavery had been addressed in my history classes, but had been treated as historical fact and not human experience. And there wasn't much talk of the immorality of slavery, of the injustices done to human beings and human bodies. *Roots* didn't just provide new information—it put the stories of embodied people in these historical events, and it turned my world upside down.

After *Roots*, I began to tear through other books that documented and humanized real-world injustices. *The Diary of Anne Frank* brought tears to my eyes; *Hiroshima* made me feel nauseous. I cried through each book and wondered what was wrong with some people that they could commit such atrocities. I couldn't believe that my country had perpetrated slavery, waited so long to respond to the Holocaust, dropped atomic bombs on Japan, and taken the land and lives of the people who had lived in America first. I was filled with so much concern for the world and such a desire for justice that I needed to find an outlet and a space to make sense of these things, if I could.

Around this time, when I was eleven years old and my parents were going through an acrimonious and disruptive divorce, some acquaintances from school invited me to accompany them to an after-school youth group hosted by a nondenominational evangelical Christian church. The church gave me what I was looking for: a safe, welcoming, grounding community during a tumultuous time in my family life and a space to explore my questions about justice. So, shortly after I started attending, I became a born-again Christian—in spite of the alien-sounding theological language of the church.

I realized two things very soon after I converted, though: I was queer, and my new church was not as welcoming as it initially seemed. This church was extremely theologically conservative and fixated on homosexuality to the point of obsession—"same-sex attraction" was mentioned in most sermons (no matter how unrelated the subject of the sermon), and there was a section of the library full of materials saying it was at best a sign of waywardness or rebellion and at worst a sign of demonic possession. I struggled profoundly with the realization that my newly realized sexual orientation and my newly adopted faith were in tension. I tried to change my sexual orientation through prayer and fasting, and when that didn't work, I became despondent and isolated.

After I had spent a few years in immense struggle, my mom discovered a prayer journal where I had detailed my inner turmoil. She took me to speak with a Christian minister at a different church. He provided a wide array of resources on Christianity and homosexuality and helped me come to terms with my sexual orientation. I moved into progressive Christian churches, finding the loving, justice-oriented community I had been seeking.

With the support and acceptance of other Christians, I came to see my earlier struggles as a way for me to better understand the experience of suffering. Still deeply concerned with building justice, I wanted to help the marginalized and disenfranchised. The people I knew who helped others the most—the people who helped me in my time of need—were pastors like the LGBTQ-affirming clergy my mother had taken me to meet with. I decided to go to a Christian college to study religion, thinking I would eventually go into Christian ministry so that I could be a supportive resource for others like the Christian mentors and ministers who had been there for me.

What I didn't fully understand then was that my desire to help others and be in community had always existed, apart from the theological claims of Christianity, and that the theology never sat easily with me. I avoided this tension for a while, but when my Christian college professors challenged me to think critically about what I believed and why I believed it, I began to realize that I had converted to Christianity at eleven years old because I sought a community that cared about justice, not because I believed in the metaphysical claims of Christianity. I had accepted the idea of God as part of a package deal because the others in my community said that God was the source of the things we cared about—community and justice—but not because I thought it made sense.

Recognizing that I was an atheist brought a kind of relief—I could finally be honest with myself—but it brought trouble, too. I felt unmoored without a community of conscience, and I struggled to discern how to relate to religious people.

In a world seemingly defined by "us against them," I no longer knew what to make of religion. I wanted to pretend that I could treat religion as a purely academic subject, observing it from a distance, but I was angry about how religion has been used to dehumanize and hurt so many people. And at a Christian college in a religiously diverse city, I was also completely surrounded by religion. My conflicted feelings about religion spilled over into my personal life, and I found it difficult to talk about religion without the discussion immediately and awkwardly devolving into the kind of argument where everyone merely recites their positions at one another and talks past one another without actually listening. As a result, I ended up struggling to connect with people who didn't share my views.

For instance, I had never really interacted with Muslims before I started volunteering at a local community center that served recent immigrants from Somalia. I had many assumptions about who they were and what they believed—and those stereotypes went mostly unchallenged because I avoided conversations about religion and atheism, maintaining a "don't ask, don't tell" posture when working at the center.

But one day, I stayed late to talk with a woman who frequented the center, and at one point, she confided in me that she was afraid to go out in public sometimes because she was frequently harassed for wearing a hijab. Immediately angry and sad about how she had been treated, I also found myself identifying with what she was describing. Without thinking, I responded by saying that though our experiences were very different, I could relate in some ways because I would get nervous when my boyfriend would hold my hand when we were out together because we had been harassed and violently attacked.

I didn't know how she would respond. I wasn't out to anyone at the center as queer and certainly not as an atheist. But without missing a beat, she asked me a question: "So what do you do in those moments, when you feel afraid?" She went on to explain that she felt strengthened by her belief that God is watching over and protecting her. "But I realize that I do not know what you believe, so I'm curious," she said. "What is your source of strength?"

To my great surprise, she didn't judge or condemn me; she didn't even flinch. Instead, she asked a question, opening a door to a different kind of conversation. She invited me to share some of my experiences, to teach her about my life as a queer person and a nontheist, and to learn more about her beliefs, identity, and experience. But I got flustered, feeling largely unable to engage religious differences in any way besides arguing, and so I changed the subject, leaving abruptly.

Eventually I began to look back on incidents like that and to see them as missed opportunities to learn, grow, and be challenged. What could happen if religious and nonreligious people had a different kind of conversation about our differences? I decided I wanted to see if I could work with religious communities to build understanding across lines of difference.

Fondly recalling the openness, curiosity, and inclusivity that I had seen modeled in my early encounters with

Unitarian Universalism, I began a master of arts in religion program at Meadville Lombard Theological School, a Unitarian Universalist seminary in Chicago. One of thirteen theological schools in the city, Meadville Lombard enabled me to cross-register at the others—an ideal situation because I wanted to study alongside, and enter into a dialogue with, many different religious people who were planning to do community-building work. I hoped to learn how they constructed meaningful moral communities.

Unfortunately, my first experiences with community groups for atheists weren't very positive. I found a kind of exclusivity and a rejection of so-called outsiders. It reminded me of my experiences in the evangelical Christian community. But I eventually found a home in Humanism, and as I began to connect with more atheists and Humanists, I became increasingly convinced that community was important to dialogue between atheists and believers. Would having more community resources enable more atheists to enter into interfaith dialogues and relationships?

Recent studies, like *American Grace* by Robert Putnam and David Campbell, suggest that the connection between religiosity and civic engagement isn't about belief; it's about belonging to a community that inspires you to reflect on what matters to you and provides you with opportunities to act on your values. They speculate that communities for Humanists could serve a similar function in equipping religiously unaffiliated people to be more civically engaged.

So communities of nonreligious nontheists are important—not only for the personal development of nonreligious individuals, but also for the common good.

In my desire to build bridges between atheists and believers—to foster dialogue and lessen the suspicion and fear both sides sometimes have for the other, to challenge the stigmas that keep us apart, and to encourage both atheists and religious believers to work together for the common good—I rediscovered the importance of community and the personal desire for a community of accountability that had initially brought me into Christianity. Because of my growing belief that nonreligious people deserve the same kinds of support and resources that religious folks have, I eventually began working at the Humanist Chaplaincy at Harvard, where I coordinated interfaith efforts and served as a chaplain. After four years there, I recently moved on to build and direct a Humanist community at Yale.

One of our members, Chelsea Link, expresses the need for communities like ours quite clearly:

> Many people go to a church or synagogue to be inspired, ask hard philosophical and ethical questions, reflect on the big picture, seek guidance and comfort in difficult times, celebrate holidays and life milestones, and join with like-minded people in community service. But nonreligious people like me often miss out on those things because we don't subscribe to the theology that goes with it. I'm so

excited to belong to the Yale Humanist Community
because it means I don't have to choose between my
beliefs and my values.

Without the support of an institution to ground and
connect them to a community and an identity, Link and
others like her miss out on many of the opportunities their
religious peers have for personal development and civic
engagement. This is perhaps particularly true for students.
When I realized as an undergraduate that I was not religious,
I felt very isolated. While my religious peers had chaplains
and communities, I felt as if I couldn't talk to anyone about
my changing beliefs, challenging experiences, and emerging
values. I felt disconnected from any community during an
important time of personal growth and discernment. I think
about that isolating feeling today whenever I meet with the
Yale Humanist Community members for pastoral care. It
reminds me how important it is that all people have access
to resources and a caring community.

For the last six years, I've worked regularly with students
at Harvard and Yale and spoken at college and university
campuses all across the United States. I've seen firsthand the
trends that are now making headlines around the world. A
2015 Pew report titled "America's Changing Religious Landscape" found that 23 percent of Americans say they are not
religious, up from 16 percent in 2007. This growth is even
more prominent among Americans under the age of thirty.

As people debate the cause of this decline, there's a more
pressing question: Where are these religiously unaffiliated

Americans finding community, connection, support, and inspiration? In particular, where are the large percentage of religiously unaffiliated millennials who say they are not looking for a religious community finding such resources? They deserve to have access to a space where they can be honest about who they are—where they can connect with others, find support, consider life's big questions, and be challenged to act on their values.

Communities of conscience and accountability play an important role in engaging people in personal reflection and moving them into civic participation, both as individuals and in partnership with other communities. The nonreligious deserve communities that can play that role for them, where their identities are respected, in a space where they can be authentically themselves.

Like religious communities, the Yale Humanist Community is an intentional moral community. We weigh and discuss questions of ultimate concern. We are bound by a shared identity that speaks to our core values. Like many religious traditions, Humanism has a rich history—and, importantly, it is an affirmational identity for those of us who are often classified by what we don't believe. Humanist communities, whether religious or nonreligious, exist to help people connect with others, find support in moments of crisis, consider life's big questions, develop humanizing relationships with other faith or moral communities, and find opportunities to act on their values.

Those of us building nonreligious communities can and should learn from the examples set by many Ethical Culture or Unitarian Universalist congregations. None of us can succeed in the work of building effective moral communities unless we are willing to learn from one another. This means looking to the many UU congregations—past and present—that have created meaningful, welcoming communities for nontheists. In talking with nonreligious people over the last six years, I've learned that many of these people are conceiving of community and identity in new and challenging ways. Our job is to listen to them and to build institutions and resources that respond to their particular needs.

Some of these resources will grow out of Unitarian Universalist spaces. Although I'm not a UU, many of my formative experiences have been in UU congregations and institutions. Others won't be connected to Unitarian Universalism at all, beyond a shared mission to create reflective, supportive communities. But I hope that UU Humanists will continue to support the burgeoning Humanist communities in all of their various shapes and forms, affirming the valuable support that people will find in non-UU Humanist communities.

◆

CHRIS STEDMAN *is the Humanist chaplain at Yale University and the author of* Faitheist: How an Atheist Found Common Ground with the Religious.